HALF OF ME

Half of Me

An Inward Journey
Back Home to Wholeness

Jennifer Gellock, PhD

This book is dedicated

to all of my family,

friends, and mentors

who have supported me

and continue to

support me

on my journey

of inner transformation

and awakening.

How to Use This Book

As you read my story, I invite you to use it as a guide into your own inner world. This book was designed to be a creative outlet for you to explore your own stories, unconscious beliefs patterns, and open-up your heart to new possibilities. This book is yours to make your own.

So, in these pages you will notice a variety of mindfulness practices I created for you to engage with. Follow the woman throughout this story and bring her once black and white world to color by using colored pencils, crayons, or other artistic expressions. Use the journal prompts to tap into your own unconscious belief patterns by letting your pen flow effortlessly as you answer the questions. Please know, there is no right or wrong way to answer these questions.

Lastly, take notes, reflect, draw, and whatever else you feel called to do as you take your own journey inward. If you connect to a particular quote, poem, or personal reflection, do not be afraid to share the beautiful design with others (shout-out to the amazing Rachel Clift) on your social media, they were designed to be *Instagramable* and shared to inspire, uplift, and normalize exploring our inner worlds.

Enjoy your journey,

Jen

CONTENTS

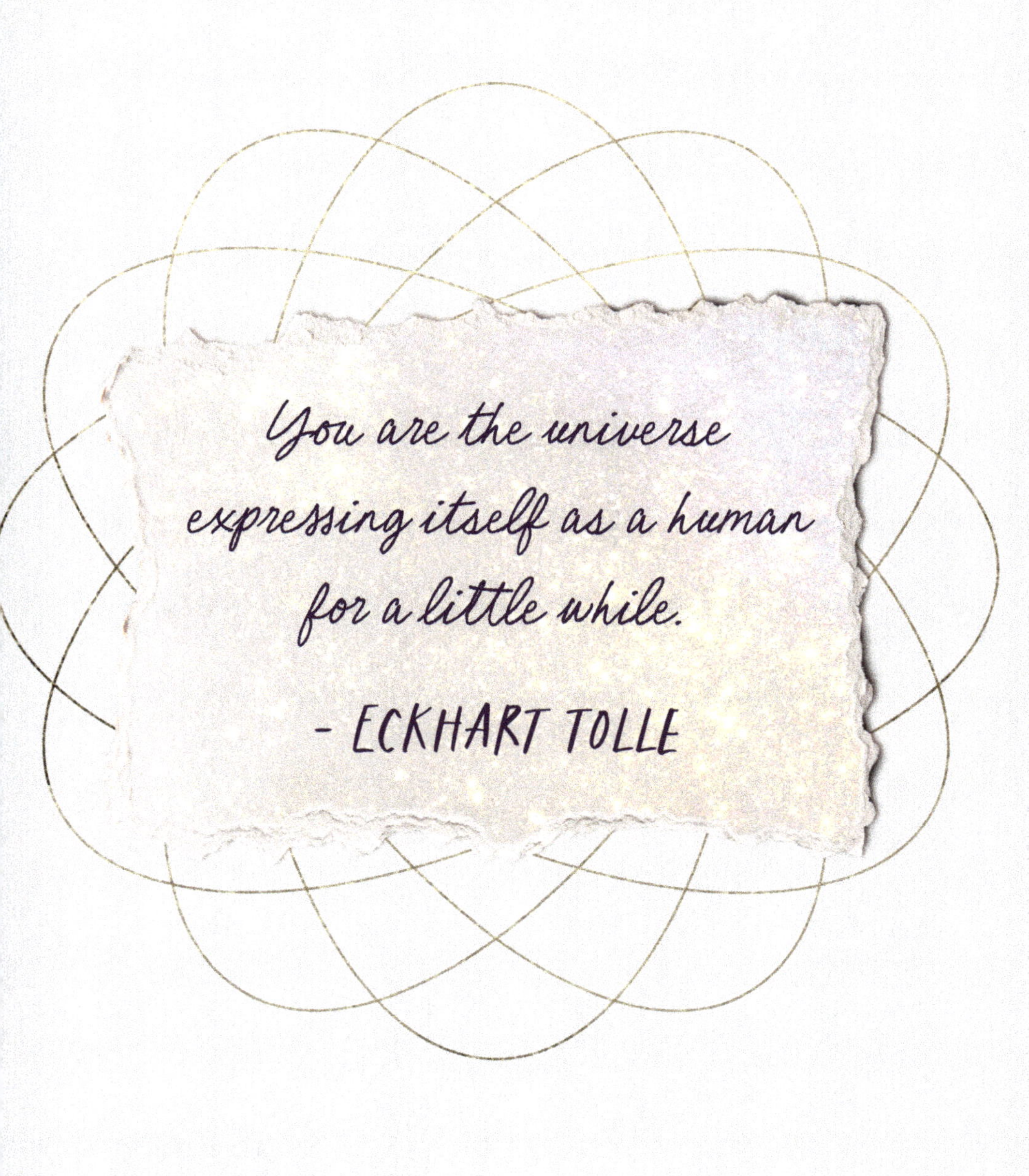

You are the universe expressing itself as a human for a little while.

- ECKHART TOLLE

Foreword

by R. Clift

*"I have met Athena. The Romans called her Minerva.
She is the caretaker of warriors, the bearer of knowl-
edge, the open hand reaching to the past, the future,
to you. She can hear the writings of past goddesses
and passes them on to the muses. I have met Athena.
She gives me courage."*

- LAURA CLIFT

I can still remember the exact moment Jen first mentioned this book to me— we were walking between ancient pillars at an enchanting *terme* in Tuscany, Italy. Under murals of healing goddesses, she told me of her vision, her tangled web of dreams and ideas that would eventually be unraveled and carefully stitched together to create the pages you hold now.

It is a rare honor to witness a poet go from the first idea for a new collection to the finished book. To have been able to stand beside Jen in this journey was a privilege beyond words. As much as I could teach the ins and outs of developing a manuscript and independently publishing a book— I know I have learned far more from just being in her presence for the past year about what it means to be an artist, a leader, and a protector. She, after all, is our Athena.

It is in reading lines such as *"Once you identify your doubts you can then use them as motivation to walk through your fears"*, and *"I have learned that the love we desire is often the love we need to give to ourselves"* when her wisdom, boundless courage, and kindness shine through to the reader. Not only are you enveloped in the guiding light of Jen's inspiring poetry, but you are invited to be a part of this book— to explore questions through journal prompts and tell your own story alongside hers.

This is a book that I invite you to return to, time and time again, for each time you read through it— something different will stand out. As you grow and evolve as a human, each chapter will speak to you in new ways. May you carry these words with you and allow yourself to be seen and understood in these pages.
May you, too, find your way *"back home to wholeness"*.

- Rachel Clift
POET, AUTHOR
May 2023

A NOTE BEFORE WE BEGIN

It is important for me to acknowledge my positionality and privilege as the author of this book. I identify as a cis-gender white female that was raised in a two-parent middle-class household.

Growing-up, my parents did all that they could to provide my sister and I with a loving home to become the women we are today. I unpack my experience of awakening through this personal lens.

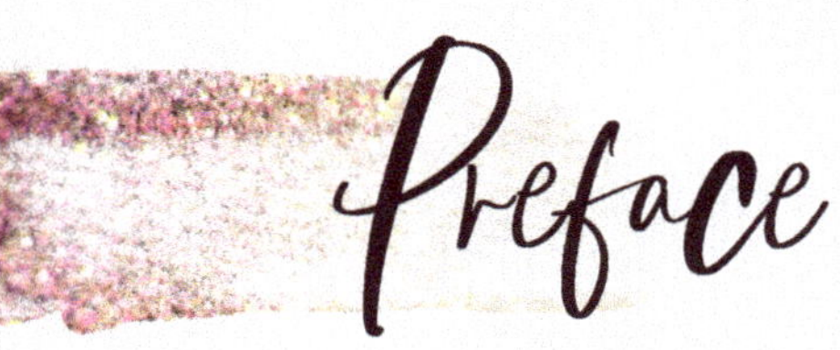

Preface

On July 27th, 2022, the idea for this book flooded my body as I walked around an ancient spa in a small town in Tuscany, Italy. I was on a trip celebrating my artistry and beginning to explore my identity as a poet after spending the prior two years on my path of awakening and journey of inner healing. On this day, I received a clear message: *it was time for me to share my journey with others.*

Back home in my apartment were ten, filled notebooks that I had accumulated from the past two years on my journey. They were filled with reflections of contemplation on how to heal my dysregulated nervous system. My daily journaling practice, somehow over time, transformed itself into poetry. And through my poetry, I learned how to come back home to my wholeness by slowly and intentionally peeling back each of my layers one by one. I can confidently say that my daily writing practice has truly healed me from the inside out.

Poetry is a powerful tool that bridges emotions (right brain) with logic (left brain). This process of integration between the right and left brain births new neural pathways to fire in ways that can lead to new beliefs that dictate new actions. Poetry can help us explore emotions like fear that can hold us in survival loops keeping us stuck in the past. And through exploration can help us transform fear into love. Looking back on my life, no one intentionally taught me how to process my own emotions.

Writing can also help us explore our unconscious belief patterns. Over the last two years, my curiosity has led me to learn about psychology and the subconscious mind. I have learned that the beliefs stored in our subconscious mind control approximately ninety-five percent of our behaviors and actions that are running our adult lives on autopilot. I have become fascinated with how the subconscious mind is developed from the time we are in the womb of our mothers to approximately ten years of age. So, unless we take the time to become aware of our internal belief patterns, we continue running on the same autopilot programming we developed throughout our childhood, which we had minimal or no control over.

So, who would you be today if you had a different upbringing? I believe becoming aware of our stories is the first step in coming back home to our wholeness. Over the last few years, I have examined every one of my thoughts, beliefs, labels, and stories by putting my pen to paper to untangle the layers of my own conditioning so that I could connect back to the truest essence of who I am. What I have learned on this journey is ready to be shared. Now is the time more than ever to tell my story through an artistic lens so that we can find our way back to wholeness together.

I hope this book takes you on your own journey to unlock doors that might be blocking the way to connect you back home to the truth of your own essence and infinite power. As I weave together my story with the art of poetry and short essays, I hope it empowers you to step into your own process of contemplation. It is my desire that this book becomes a safe space for you to be cradled in self-love as you take your own journey inward. In each part of this book, you will be invited to practice some mindfulness exercises of reading, reflection, and coloring. If you have a curious mind and a hand to write with, this book is for you.

Thank you for being here.

If you're ready, *it's time to go inward.*

I'm not meant to be here long

I'm just here to collect
all the things
I've left behind

To reclaim
all the parts of myself
that I cut off in an effort
just to be loved

It's only in walking back these paths
that I get to reclaim
all of these small pieces

I know I'm here
until I can love myself
back into wholeness

So, I choose to take
this journey inward
and welcome all
of me back home

To let the love of God
stream through me
and collect what
I had once forgotten

I'm here for a soul retrieval

In the summer of 2021, I moved back to Tampa, FL for what I thought was my dream job. Tampa was a place that always has felt like home to me and it was a city I always wanted to return back to. I wrote this poem after my first one-on-one session working with my transformational coach and mentor, Aaron Rose in February of 2022. It was this poem that opened a gateway for me to further explore my spiritual path and step into what I now call my divine mission and what I believe to be the true reason I was brought back to Tampa. I came back for a soul retrieval.

Jen

i'm here for a soul retrieval

part i.

Life Pivots

"When do you know it is the right time
to make a pivot in your life?
I believe there is no right way to logically
arrive at a clear answer to this question.
First, you must get quiet enough to tap
into your own inner wisdom long enough
to let your intuition whisper and lead you
in the right direction forward.
Then, you must build up enough courage
to take a leap of faith.

When your intuition speaks,
I hope you don't ignore it—

I hope you pivot."

On Monday, October 10, 2022, I walked into the Department Chair's office at the University of Tampa and told them I would not be returning to my role as a tenure-track Assistant Professor of Sport Management the following academic year. At the age of thirty-three, I was back at the place that shaped me as an undergrad now there I was, serving a new generation of students. This was the hardest decision I have ever had to make in my entire life. When I accepted the position, I believed it was my dream job. It had a secure career trajectory, it fulfilled my passion for teaching, and I was at an institution that has always felt like home to me.

However, from the very first time I stepped foot back on that campus, in my new role, *something did not feel right.* The prior two years up to this point, I was in a deep portal of inner transformation. I was navigating a spiritual awakening and coming back home to the truth of what I believe I am here to do and how I am meant to serve during this lifetime.

Looking back, I have always honored myself by making hard decisions to better my future which has always moved me closer to my true calling. The decision to leave academia felt like the ultimate honor of my soul's mission forward. For all of the pivot points I had taken up until this moment in my life, I had no conscious idea I was being guided closer to aligning with my greater purpose. However, I know now, that there was always an intuitive knowing nudging me back to my own truth all along. I believe the universe, God, our higher self (or however you connect with your truth) truly wants us to become the most authentically expressed versions of ourselves and will continue to send us signs and tiny miracles along our path to shift us back home in that direction. There are a few pivot points in my life that stand out most to me.

At the age of eighteen, I decided to go to college at the University of Tampa, over a thousand miles away from where I grew up in Westfield, Massachusetts. I chose this institution because it had a good Sport Management program and a pool on campus. I remember my mom saying, "if you don't like it, you can always come home." When I got to school, I remember having a rough time adjusting to my freshman year because I had no idea how to make friends without playing sports. I had played sports in every season for my whole life growing up and I always had a built in friend group in my teammates because of that. So, I did the only thing I knew how and walked myself over to the athletic department and asked if there was anything I could do to get involved in. I spent the next four years working in athletics in the sports information department and joining the women's basketball team as a student manager. I ended up graduating college Magna Cumme Laude with a degree in K-12 Physical Education, but after completing my student teaching I learned that it was just not the right path for me.

So I pivoted.

At the age of twenty-two, I accepted my first full-time job as an Assistant Women's Basketball Coach at Saint Leo University. After two successful years, the head coach I was working under transitioned out of her role unexpectedly, and I felt blindsided and lost. I was presented with two choices: either stay in my job working for the next hired head coach or leave with no plan. I decided to take inventory of all the things that were working and not working in my life as an assistant coach. My parents desperately wanted me to stay. They were always my biggest fans growing up as an athlete and then as a coach. However, I came to the conclusion that what I loved most about coaching was working with my players off the court and hearing about their hopes, dreams, and plans for their futures after their competitive playing careers came to an end. It was hard to accept that I wasn't on the right path, but I decided to follow my inner guidance system anyways.

So I pivoted.

I tell my students and clients today to always say "yes" to the things that are pulling them forward even if they don't know what will be on the other side of that experience. Every time I have said "yes," I have been able to use that experience to learn something new, meet new people, or help me clarify my own path ahead. With my MBA in Sport Business in hand, I ended up taking a part-time role at Central Michigan University in their Student-Athlete Services Department just to get my foot in the door.

At the age of twenty-four, I found myself in the middle of the state of Michigan where I didn't know anyone or much at all about the University. I was eager to learn and work for a NCAA Division I Athletic Department and serve student-athletes competing at an elite level. I showed up every day, working extra hours because my worth at the time depended on the validation I received from others for my hard work and hustle. After one year, I was quickly promoted to a full-time position when yet again, I was presented with another choice to make. I quickly began to lack resonance with the collegiate athletic system and was learning that in order to move up in the profession one day I would possibly be faced with compromising my own integrity when working with high profile teams and coaches. I was learning that "athlete" oftentimes became prioritized before "student" at this level of athletics and it was not something I agreed with.

I began to investigate other career paths that connected me to my interests in teaching, serving, and being a curious-minded individual. I began doing informational interviews with Ph.D. students and professors I knew on campus. Ultimately, I was intrigued as to why some of my track and field athletes had no idea what they wanted to do after their college athletic careers came to an end. The few short years I spent working in the high-pressure environment of college athletics had me asking a lot of questions about athletic identity and what happens next for athletes in their life after playing organized sports at an elite level. I believed pursuing a path of research as an academic would be a good next step.

So I pivoted.

At the age of twenty-seven, I was accepted at Virginia Commonwealth University (VCU) as a full-time Doctoral Student and Teaching and Research Assistant for the Center for Sport Leadership where I was guided by the most supportive mentors. During this time, I operated from the same hustle-and-grind mentality I did in my twenties. In 2019, I defended my dissertation, *Work-life Factors that Impact Job Burnout and Turnover Intentions Among Academic Support Professionals* when a few years later, job burnout manifested in my own life in a very real way. It was there at VCU during my graduate experience and classes where I began having conversations of intersectionality and confronting my own privileges for the very first time. Not only did I learn about the identities of athletes but I became even more curious of my own. After three years, I took my first full-time job as an Assistant Professor in Sport Management at the University of North Alabama and my dream job opened up just two years later back at the University of Tampa, a place I always wanted to return to.

Looking back, it has been a beautiful path forward to where I am now. However, throughout all of these experiences in my twenties, I was living with unmanaged chronic stress and anxiety. I always felt like I was fighting to overcome imposter syndrome, questioning if I was doing the right thing, and feeling unfulfilled in my overall day-to-day life. I was often left paralyzed in fight or flight disassociated from my body and there were many days I did not want to get out of bed. I would often spend my weekends letting my body rest to recover as a byproduct of hustling through resistance during the previous week. However, I always dreamed there was something more heart-opening and purposeful out there for me.

I am now thirty-three years old and I find myself yet again at another pivot point. However, this change in my life feels different. It feels more true than anything I have ever known before because I believe it aligns with a higher calling that can't be explained, only deeply known.

So I'm pivoting.

"we often become who we think we need to be in order to be loved"

WHO HAVE YOU HAD TO BECOME IN ORDER TO FEEL LOVED?

SHE SCREAMS

ACTIVATING THE UNHEARD VIBRATIONS
OF HER VOICE

ONCE SCARED TO SPEAK UP
AND DELIVER HER TRUTH

HER VOCAL CORDS
RUSTED OVER
FROM YEARS OF SILENCE

DECADES
OF UNSPOKEN WORDS
LODGED WITHIN HER THROAT

SHE SCREAMS

NOW EACH MORNING
SHE SOAKS HERSELF
WITH LIQUID HONEY

SOFTENING THE HURT
WITH EVERY RELEASE
THAT ROLLS OFF HER TONGUE

ON HER OWN TERMS
SHE DECIDES
IT'S TIME TO TELL HER STORY

ALL OF IT

HALF OF ME

it's
time
to tell
her
story

half of me

There are a million half-written poems
in half-filled notebooks
stacked on shelves
that I put a half-assed effort into building

And within all these poems
lies only half my heart

Because I wrote them
from half-felt emotions
stemming from
my half-lived human life

Honestly
I think for when you read my words
you'd only learn half
of who I truly am

It's just like when my friends
pick up the phone to call me
and I only tell them half the truth
so I burden them
with only half my hurt

And sometimes I wonder
if half of anything
will ever be enough

I mean, it must be
because I have heard the stories
of people who have traveled
halfway around the world
to meet the loves of their lives
against all odds

And those who see the glass half-full
referred to as the optimistic ones

And even under the light
of a half-lit moon

there's still enough energy
to pull the tides
that sustains the rhythm
of all our human lives

But if I'm being truly honest
I think I've always known
that half of anything
will never be enough

Because when I hold
myself back
I know I'm only
halfway to freedom

I've learned
that half-filled promises
will only break others hearts

And that half-lived dreams
won't move me closer
to fulfilling my ultimate destiny

Honestly
I think for when my last day
comes to live
I think I'd be sad
if I completed only half
my Earthly tasks

Now

there are a million half-written poems
in half-filled notebooks
stacked on shelves
that I put a half-assed effort into building

And at the heart
of all of these half done things
I've finally learned
it was just the fear of being fully seen

"I began writing daily
in the summer of 2020
as an effort to heal
my nervous system.
Not only did it heal
my nervous system, but
it also ended up
healing my heart."

Without being too dramatic
poetry has saved my life
more times than I can count

I took the pain
that lived inside my chest
and transformed it into magical words

Each turning of a page
pulled me up from
the bottom of the ocean
with a tenacity of a cat
clawing its way up a tree

Writing was a lifeline
thrown to me by a God
I had yet to believe in

And with each letter
that made its way through my pen
the energy that connected me
to an infinite Source
became clearer and clearer

I held steady as each page I wrote
began to unwind the knots
from within me

I kept turning and turning
until I could touch
the truth of my soul
with just this ink

Now, I touch the truth
of my soul everyday
because I choose to write

WHAT ARE THINGS THAT BRING YOU BACK TO LIFE?

Do you allow yourself
to do these things enough?

SHE IS READY
TO HEAL

TO KNOW WHAT
IT'S LIKE
TO FEEL SAFE
IN HER
OWN BODY
AGAIN

TO SOOTH HER BATTLE
OF LIVING IN A BODY
THAT ONLY KNOWS
A LIFE OF LIVING IN
FIGHT OR FLIGHT

SHE'S READY
TO COME BACK HOME
TO THE PEACE

SHE'S READY
TO COME BACK
HOME TO WHOLENESS

"to heal it
you must feel it"

2020 to 2022

Two years
of solitude
preparing me
for every single yes
about to come
my way

As I came home
to myself
I learned the essence
of my spirit

Each day
I took a new journey
inward

I leaned into each
and every
present moment

As God
molded me
with patience

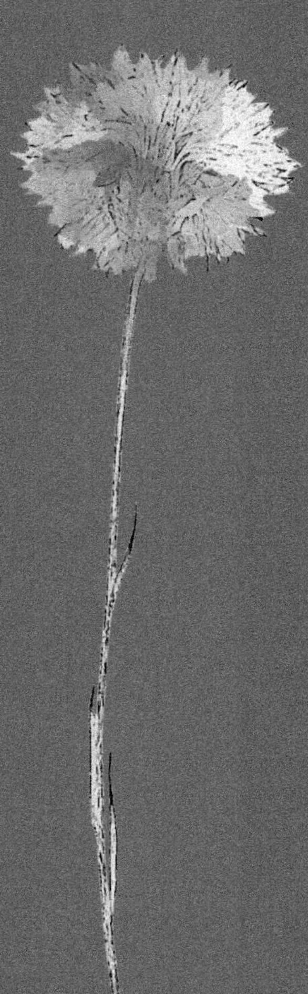

He sits across from me
and I know he's looking at me
wondering what it is
that I'm writing

But rather than tell him
what I'm writing
I'd rather tell him
why I write

Because the energy coursing underneath
the *why I write*
is so much more important
than the *what*

So, if he walks over to me
and asks
what I will tell him is

Upon waking each day
I write to set my intentions
towards the rising sun

So that the light of day
carries me to meet
all the right people
in all the right places

I write to capture
tiny miracle moments
that take my breath away

So that I can hold their essence
in a time capsule
of my notebook forever

Clasped inside these lined pages
are where I have poured
my heart out in remembrance

The remembrance
of my divine mission
here on Earth

And he may think it's crazy but
what I will tell him is

I write to rewrite the stories housed
in the subconscious of my mind
the ones that serve me no good
to hold onto any longer

To rewrite the beliefs
that have long ago expired
so that I can shift
my mirrored reality
convincing myself
that I am worthy

Worthy of being seen
for my creativity
and worthy of being loved
for just who I am

A writer

I write to express words
I can't just yet say out loud
because I know that
once they find this page
they seem less scarier
to share with another

I can even share them
with a crowd

I write in order to feel
these heavy emotions
to transmute memories
that have built up inside me over time
and move them through me

 HALF OF ME

So that I can finally let them go
and say goodbye
to what no longer serves me

Writing is my daily ritual
and communion with God

And before I lay my head
on my pillow at night
I bring forth gratitude
with my pen
so that I don't forget
where I came from
or where I'm going
and to remind myself
that when you find
what you're meant to be doing
there just isn't any other option

So I write

He walks over to me
and he asks me
what it is that I'm writing

And I respond
If you have the time
I'd rather tell you why I write

"One of my favorite teachers on leadership, Simon Sinek, said, *People don't buy what you do, they buy why you do it.* I have learned that intentions are powerful declarations that shape our beliefs which inspire our actions. They ripple an energy into the world creating the manifestations in our lives that impact the world around us. So I encourage you to become intentional with your actions and bring awareness to your *why*. You may be surprised just what you can consciously create."

WHAT IS YOUR *Why* FOR GETTING OUT OF BED EACH MORNING?

SHE GOT LOST
INSIDE THE PAGES
OF HER JOURNAL

WRAPPED INSIDE
THE YEARS OF WRITING
YOU WILL FIND
THE JOURNEY
SHE HAS WALKED
FROM THE WOMAN
SHE ONCE WAS
TO THE WOMAN
SHE'S NOW BECOMING

SHE TRAVERSED
OVER PEAKS
AND DOWN THROUGH VALLEYS
TREKKING OVER
THE TERRAIN
OF HER ONCE
BROKEN HEART

MEETING ANGELS
ON HER TRAVELS
THAT HELPED SMOOTH
HER CRACKED SHELL
BACK TOGETHER AGAIN

AND ON THE DAY
WHEN THEY LAID
HER DOWN TO REST
SHE WAS FOUND
INSIDE THE PAGES
OF HER JOURNAL

 HALF OF ME

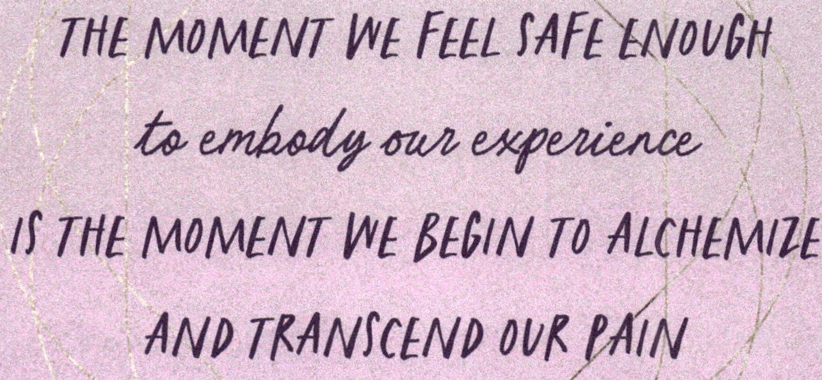

THE MOMENT WE FEEL SAFE ENOUGH
to embody our experience
IS THE MOMENT WE BEGIN TO ALCHEMIZE
AND TRANSCEND OUR PAIN

In between the liberation
of your old story
and trusting your new one
are monsoons of grief

One day
I will write a whole book
about the grief

The grief
that one goes through
when dying to an old self

The death that's required
to expand into new versions
of yourself

Grief is threaded throughout
all of our expansion

For example:
For flowers to bloom again in the spring
they must first die in the fall
and grieve all of the winter
when they were not yet a flower

One day
I will write
a whole book
about the grief

"There are five themes in this book:
liberation, connection, creativity,
surrender, and trust.
The theme of grief deserves
its own book one day.
I have had many ego deaths
along my transformational journey
thus far and I am guessing there will
be many more to come.
Each surrender to an old identity
has required the death of my ego
which was accompanied by
its own wave of grief.
One day, I will write a whole book about
the grief one will go through
when commiting to a process
of inner transformation."

Who Would You Be if You Released All of the Stories of Who You Think You Should Be?

part ii.

Liberation

I made my first vision board in January 2020 out of desperation. I was searching for any-thing that would help me feel connected to myself and a life of more joy, fulfillment, and peace. I was willing to do anything to find my way out of my anxious-depressive loops that had encased me for most of my twenties. One day I took magazines from a co-worker and spread them out all over my apartment floor. I had no idea what I was doing as I began ripping out pictures and words as I was being guided by my intuition. And in the middle of the collage, I cut and pasted letter by letter the word: *l-i-b-e-r-a-t-e.*

Liberate spoke to me that new year as my one-word intention. I remember, during that season of my life, the expression, *the weight of the world on my shoulders,* being an all too real feeling that was only building more with each passing day. I remember desperately wanting to feel lighter in my mind, in my body, and in my spirit. I just didn't know how to get there. That's when all the years of chronic stress from suppressing my emotions from living life out of alignment became too much.

On August 10, 2020, I began to panic as nausea started to roll through my whole body. My chest began to tighten, my heart began palpitating faster and faster and my breathing became shallow. Pain began to radiate as it shot up the side of my left arm into my jaw as an impending doom of death catapulted me to pick up the phone and call my sister Jamie to tell her that "I thought that I was having a heart attack".

When she answered the phone I told her, "I think that I am going to die." As I began to cry, I ran to the bathroom thinking I was either going to blackout or throw up. My sister encouraged me to call a friend nearby. So, I called my neighbor Melissa who graciously came over to help try to ease my mind and tell me as non-judgmentally as she could, "I think you're just having anxiety." The same thing my sister had told me. "You don't understand," I told both of them. "I have lived with anxiety my whole life and this is something very different."

That night, Melissa kindly drove me to the emergency room to get checked out. I went again a few days later with the same symptoms. On each visit, I was sent home and told they couldn't find anything wrong with my heart, and that they thought "I was just having anxiety." I ended up going to see a family physician after my trips to the emergency room to get a full workup done, and again was told that, "they couldn't find anything wrong with me and they thought I was just having anxiety."

The summer of 2020 was one of the first times in my life my body was not in "go, go, go" mode because there was nowhere to go during the societal shutdown of the global pandemic. And my body did not know how to react and slow down with the world around it. Not only did I experience panic attacks on a very human level, but over the course of that week, my spirit moved as I prayed to God for the first time in my life, asking for the reprieve from the weight I had been feeling. I had a profound transcendental experience where I aligned with the truth of an all consuming love that I can only describe as God. *I will discuss this more in detail in another part of this book.*

Today, I look back, and I am amazed by the synchronicities of the universe. Or maybe it was just a self-fulfilling prophecy. Either way, it was the medicine I needed to begin my healing journey. Because just one year prior in 2019, I had defended my dissertation for the completion of my Ph.D. on the topic of job burnout. And there I was myself, completely depleted, emotionally exhausted with a dysregulated nervous system, and becoming resentful of my job and the students I was there to serve. I was exhibiting all of the symptoms I had previously researched about how job burnout manifests itself. I was always interested in how people lived happy and fulfilled lives but never actually fully adopted the practices to be integrated into my own life.

I lived most of my life coping and self-managing chronic stress and anxiety. I attribute my chronic stress and anxiety to operating from overdeveloped masculine energy that manifested as a result of my conditioning growing up in a patriarchal society that values masculine energetic traits. People of all gender identities have both masculine and feminine energy flowing through them. Masculine energy is described as more achievement-focused, dedicated, structured, and goal oriented, while feminine energy is described as more intuitive, creative, compassionate, and nurturing. I believe integrating the masculine and feminine energies within us is what allows for our true expression to be unleashed. As a society, we celebrate and value the masculine energy qualities in both men and women as leaders. Throughout my whole twenties, when I wasn't in my masculine energy, I would feel guilty for not moving toward external achievements and outward successes. A lot of my overdeveloped masculine energy I acquired through my conditioning as an athlete and working as a professional in a win-at-all-costs sport culture.

I carried my athlete mindset with me well into my professional career, and working in the environment of college athletics only amplified my unhealthy relationship with masculine energy. I overworked myself most of my twenties by adapting to the twenty-four-seven work culture of college athletics and continued this lifestyle into graduate school completing my doctorate degree in three years. However, working at this pace never felt truly right. I put so much pressure on myself because I believed that in order to "win" was to meet the expectations someone else set for me and to reach some external accolade. I never learned how to drop into and integrate into my core feminine energy and source my worth from inside myself until after my panic attacks in 2020. While I have now learned that pressure can be beneficial and provide discomfort needed to transform, expand, and take action, I was doing too much, too soon, for my nervous system to hold it all at one time. Couple this with not understanding how to process my own emotions (which are just energy in motion), and I was a pressure cooker waiting to pop.

Since the summer of 2020, I have been on a journey of learning how to self-regulate my nervous system and learning how to feel healthy in my mind, body, heart, and spirit. Some spiritual teachers call what I have been going through, a spiritual awakening that leads you into a dark night of the soul. This experience has left me seeking to learn more about how to dissolve my false identities, align back with my truth, and reclaim my relationship with myself and with God. I have been on a wild healing journey connecting back home to myself and now I want to help others do the same.

SHE DOESN'T KNOW
WHERE HER HOME IS ANYMORE

HER ROOTS WERE PULLED
FROM THE EARTH
A LONG TIME AGO
TO WEATHER
THE WINTER

SO SHE JOURNEYED
THROUGH THE COLD
TO FIND A NEW HOME

A PLACE TO FINALLY
BE NOURISHED
BY THE WARMTH
OF THE SUN

SEARCHING FOR REFUGE
AFFORDING HER
THE OPTIMAL CONDITIONS
TO GROW IN

SO THAT SHE COULD
BLOOM AGAIN
ONCE THE SPRING RETURNED

HALF OF ME

"i used to believe

people only

loved me

when i was

struggling"

I think most
will call me crazy
too privileged
for my own good

A Ph.D.
thrown out
on the streets
starting over
on new dreams

Still holding
onto so much shame
for deciding
to leave

It's been lingering
in my heart's chambers
for years

But you see
I was headed
towards burnout

Beginning to
depersonalize others

Struggling to dethrone
this heavy weight
off my shoulders

Unsure
if I was even
qualified anymore

Seeking the feeling
of freedom

Just wanting
to breathe again

All along there
was a new truth emerging
And I couldn't ignore
it any longer

My soul-mission alive
and in living color
waiting for me and
calling me forward

In 2019 I defended my dissertation on the topic of Job Burnout
and in 2020 it became my lived-reality.

Jen

Stable

consistent

a dependable part of me

always on edge

searching for every exit

avoiding intimate connection

looking to run

heart out on loan

it's all in my head

detached from my body

limbs tingling with numbness

heart pounding

chest getting tighter

compressing my lungs

clenched jaw

fists in a ball

HALF OF ME

standing on guard

defending a false self

controlled by a victimized mentality

searching for love in all the wrong places

living inside a box

no way out

trapped

getting claustrophobic

still searching for an exit

always on edge

a dependable part of me

consistent

stable

hello nice to meet you

    I'm anxious

"I lived in a state of chronic stress
with a dysregulated nervous system
all of my twenties.
This is what my day to day
felt like most of the time.
Writing has been one of the tools
to help me heal and
bring my nervous system
back into balance.
It is now a tool I use
to help guide others back home
to their own inner peace."

reminder:
you
are not
your
anxious
thoughts

WHAT THOUGHTS OF YOURS ARE EXPIRED?

HALF OF ME

AT A YOUNG AGE
SHE LEARNED
TO TURN OFF
HER FEELINGS

OVER TIME
BECOMING NUMB
TO THE WORLD
AROUND HER

SCARED TO FEEL
HER OWN
BEATING HEART
AND EVEN MORE TERRIFIED
TO LET ANOTHER
COME CLOSE ENOUGH
TO BREAK IT

SHE HAD AN ELECTRIC FENCE
OF PERFECTIONISM
ENTANGLED
WITH HER AURA

UNABLE TO FEEL
FULLY ALIVE
INSIDE HER
OWN BODY

AVOIDING THE DEMONS
THAT MADE HER TEMPLE
THEIR HOME

HOWEVER
DEEP DOWN
SHE KNEW

THE ONLY WAY
TO LIVE AGAIN
*WAS TO FEEL THEM
AND RELEASE THEM*

 HALF OF ME

I thought
I made it

Through the years
of hustle
years of struggle
meeting the measures
of a successful life

Applying the mentality of
*what doesn't kill you
makes you stronger*

But I found out
a little bit too late
that statement only applies
to those
whose souls are
lit on fire
with their mission

"I have learned that
when I am lit on fire
with my soul's mission,
I can accomplish more
than I ever thought I could.
But doing all of the things
that are not meant for me
will lead me to burnout."

SHE SAID
*I KNOW THERE IS SOMETHING MORE
OUT THERE FOR ME*

*MORE THAN THIS NINE-TO-FIVE GRIND
MORE THAN WAKING UP EVERY DAY
WISHING SOMETHING
WOULD CHANGE*

*MORE THAN A
RINSE AND REPEAT
KIND OF DAY AFTER DAY*

SHE SAID
*I KNOW THERE IS SOMETHING MORE
OUT THERE FOR ME*

*I'VE SPENT MY WHOLE LIFE
WATCHING OTHERS CHASE THEIR DREAMS
NEVER THINKING IT COULD BE ME*

SHE SAID
*I KNOW THERE IS SOMETHING MORE
OUT THERE FOR ME*

*I'M FINALLY READY
TO CREATE MY LIFE*

*I'M NOT SURE YET
HOW TO DO IT
OR WHERE I'M GOING
BUT I AM READY TO FIND OUT*

Jello without a mold
a clock that can't keep time
no more gas left in the tank
a dammed river
melancholy melodies
weeping willow trees
colorblind mice
the last one picked for kickball
fogged-up mirrors
faking it till you make it
avoiding the inevitable
icing the kicker
a broken smile
snag in my tights
stale chips
soggy socks
flat Soda
sugar crash
plastic cover on my nana's couch
sweaty palms
teeth colliding on an awkward first kiss
my missing puzzle piece
a broken water heater
only cold showers
misplaced keys
a yellow spot of snow
no plot line or
fairy tale ending
a slow death of my soul
I'm out of alignment

Thank you to those who contributed some lines to this poem when I asked them,
"How would you describe what it's like when you're not feeling like your best self?"

    HALF OF ME

Jen

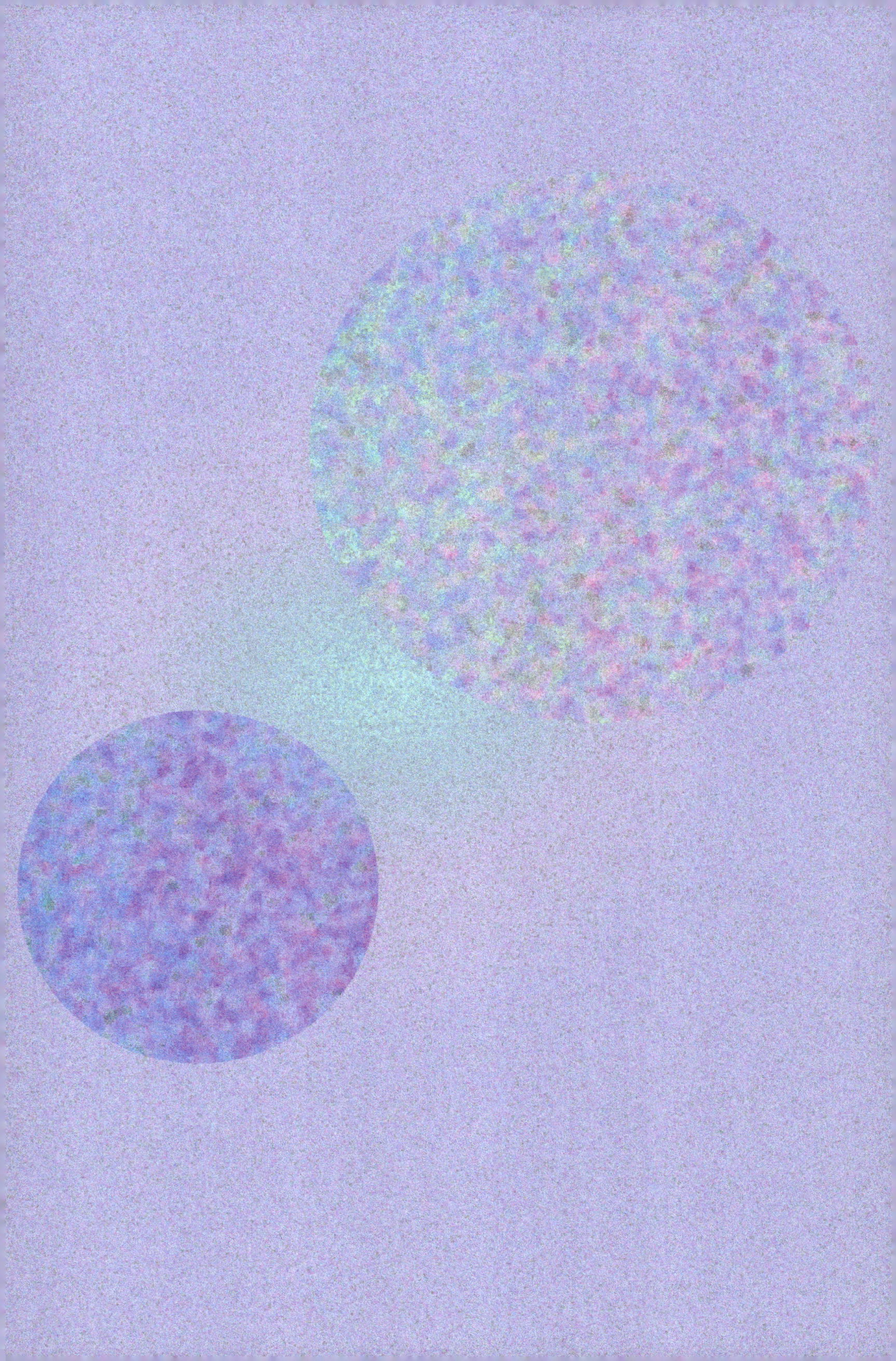

SHE PEOPLE-PLEASED
HER WAY
ALL THE WAY
TO THE TOP
OF THE MOUNTAIN

WHEN SHE MADE IT
TO THE SUMMIT
OVERLOOKED THE EDGE
AND CAST HER VISION
UPON THE HORIZON

HER SATISFACTION FELL FLAT

BECAUSE SHE REALIZED
IN THAT MOMENT
HOW SHE HAD CLIMBED
THE WHOLE FUCKING MOUNTAIN FOR THEM

AND NEVER TOOK

ONE

SINGLE

STEP

FOR

HERSELF

They may never know the real me

I said to him
as I placed my head
in my hands
bursting at the seams
sobbing glittered tears of grief
angry in this realization

Is it that they never cared to listen?

Or did they skip the part to
even ask the questions?

I just wish someone would have asked me

Are you happy?

Who do you want to be?

What does your heart want to create today?

Round and round
feeding into the societal assumptions
of who they think
I should be

Is it my fault
for failing to express myself?

I look back
and I'm confused

How did I get here?

They're still not listening

HALF OF ME

Afraid of who I'm becoming
drifting away slowly
deviating from that straight and narrow path
that I was good at staying in

Maybe they were scared
my wings were broken

Their hearts were in the right place
just wanting to protect me

Yet, they were pinning me down
before I ever had the chance
to take flight

Attempting
to keep me
safely grounded

But you see

I'm no bird

I'm a fish

Now swimming in a sea
of forgiveness
no longer fighting upstream
I'm headed down

I've decided
they don't need to know me

So I set myself free
and splashed
into the unknown

"I grew up feeling like no one
truly understood me.
So, I tried my whole life to fit in
to feel like I belonged.
I found myself always trying
to fix myself to be like others.
However, I still was never truly happy.
Brene Brown says,
the opposite of fitting in is belonging.
This makes sense to me.
I have come to learn and
rewrite a new belief that being me;
a highly sensitive, intuitive, and creative
person is who I'm meant to be
and on the day I felt like I belonged
to myself, was the day I stopped trying
to fit in."

 HALF OF ME

WHERE IN YOUR LIFE
ARE YOU TRYING TO FIT IN?

> When you begin to belong to yourself.
> You no longer will feel the need to fit in.

I've traveled
across the world
to SouthEast Asia

Down to the
southern tip
of Africa

Across the pond
to Europe

Sailed the countries
of the Caribbean

However
the most adventurous journey
I have ever taken

Has been making the trip
from my head
to my heart

I can't be the fullest expression
of myself here
any longer
I've outgrown
these four walls
I once slumbered in

Left inside this box
that continues to shrink
around me

I've stayed too long
and now I'm stuck

I'm beginning
to get claustrophobic

Expanding my awareness
at a rapid rate

At the precipice
of wanting to jump free
off this cliff

It's time
to break free

I can
hardly
breathe

Sometimes I think
it might be easier
to stay

But if I do
I might just suffocate

And I'd rather not die
a slow death
inside this box

HALF OF ME

This box
That I was taught to live inside of
by others

It's no longer a choice

My whole body is telling me
it's time to go

Yet my brain keeps saying
it's safer to stay

And I've abandoned the intuition
stored inside my body
too many times to know

What it would cost me to stay

And It might
just cost me
my life

So I told them
I love you so much
But it's time
for me
to go

After I wrote this poem, it became clear to me that it was time to move on and leave academia. It was now time for me begin a new chapter of my life teaching outside the walls of the traditional higher education system and find truer alignment.

Jen

TO REWIRE MY BELIEFS THAT NO LONGER SERVED ME

I HAD TO LIFT THEM OUT OF THE DARKNESS

reexamine their meanings in my life

AND THEN RE-PATCH THEM BACK TOGETHER

WITH LOVE AND LIGHT FROM INSIDE MY HEART

SHE CLIMBED
STEP BY STEP
DOWN A GOLDEN LADDER

TO THE BOTTOM OF A CAVE
WHERE SHE MET
A WALL OF MIRRORS

COMING FACE TO FACE
WITH HER OWN
REFLECTED SHADOW

IT WAS THERE
THAT SHE LIFTED HER GAZE
TO MEET A HALLOWED VERSION
OF A WOMAN SHE
ONCE KNEW

FOR TOO MANY YEARS
SHE TRIED TO NEVER LOOK
HER SHADOW IN THE EYE

BUT THIS TIME
WAS DIFFERENT

SHE REMEMBERED
THERE COULD NEVER
BE A SHADOW
WITHOUT THE LIGHT

SO SHE TOOK HER SHADOW
BY THE HAND TO CLIMB TOGETHER
BACK OUT OF THE CAVE

TO CLIMB
BACK OUT
TOWARDS
THE
SUN

a letter to myself: the poet

They will call you pretentious
just another poet
with nothing meaningful to say
as they watch you deliver a poem
from your heart
they'll still judge you
for every single word
then point to what they believe
is the egoic nature
of your art

You'll ask questions
when you first get started like
*why can't they see me
when I bare my naked soul?*

If it wasn't for them to receive
maybe they could have
just walked away
and never said a thing

They have no clue
how long it took you
to get here
to claim your title
as poet

But what if they are right?
as you find yourself
amidst another
self-assigned label

Another box
you swore you'd never package
yourself inside of
Just another crystal castle

that you decided
to live inside the walls of

And it could surely crack
with just one doubtful opinion
of another

But you see
you are more
than any label
or box
to be put in

I hope you always remember
there is no way
that you could ever be
just one thing

So the next time
you tell that person
who cast skepticism your way
thank you for this humble reminder

*I am indeed no poet
I am a queen
of all artistic things*

*I am a dancer in the kitchen
to Motown beats
dancing just as spicy
as I like to make my fajitas*

*And I am a painter
on my living room floor
brushing color into the visions
of my dreams in the future*

And I am a singer
in the shower
a place where I'm the star
of my own casted
American Idol

And I am a lover
when the sun goes down
making magic between the sheets
every time he sets
my soul on fire

So no, ma'am
I am no a poet
I am a queen of
all artistic things

"People will always have
their opinions of you.
How can you use them
as a point of reflection
for where you might still
be doubting yourself?
Once you identify your doubts
you can then use them
as motivation to walk through
your fears."

It's time to forgive myself

For all the times I starved myself
of life giving moments
and all the times
I over indulged in them

For all the times I ran
when there was nothing to run from
and all the times
I stayed when there was

For all the times I lied
to save my reputation
and all the times
I told the truth
to those who never earned it

For all the times I held in my anger
when I should have expressed it
and all the times
I unleashed it on loved ones
who never ever deserved it

For all the times I was right
and didn't speak my truth
and all the times
I was wrong
and chose to speak out of line

For all the times I fought
with all my might and lost
and all the times
I threw in the towel
when I could have stayed in the ring

For all the choices I made too quickly
and got burned by the fire
and all the times
I waited too long
and I let the perfect
moment pass me by

For all the times
I burned the midnight oil
and stayed out too long
and for all the times
I left too early
and missed the shooting star

For all the times I loved too hard
and the times I chose to run away

I forgive myself for it all

WHAT ARE THE THINGS IN YOUR LIFE THAT HAVE BEEN HOLDING YOU BACK THAT YOU ARE READY TO LET GO OF?

HALF OF ME

Creativity

In the summer of 1999, you could find me lip-synching to Stacy's Mom and can-nonballing into our four-foot-deep oval pool. I remember spending that whole summer running around with a Sony digital camcorder, capturing moments with the intention to make others laugh. I was both the director and the producer of a variety of projects. I choreographed music videos, staged funny stunts, and captured moments for my future application to one day be on the cast of a reality TV show like *Survivor* or *Fear Factor*. Growing up, the freest I ever felt was when I was creating with no boundaries or limits. However, I only remember being in this specific creative energy during my summer and winter breaks off of school.

I remember school providing me with minimal opportunities to be creative. When in class, I spent my time daydreaming to be somewhere else creating outside the walls of the traditional classroom. One experience during my freshman year of high school, in the only art class I remember being required to take, we got assigned to paint a self-portrait of ourselves using a photograph of our choice. I chose a picture of myself beaming ear to ear with a smile, in my prom dress, holding my wiener dog, Artie. I remember enjoying that art class so much that it became something I looked forward to attending each day that semester.

In the final painting, I had the proportions a bit off and my body looked a few sizes larger than the accurate dimensions, but I still remember being really proud of the final painting. And when I brought it home to share it with my family, it ended up being quite a running joke that brought many laughs for many years, as it sat on the mantle of my childhood home's fireplace for the rest of my high school career. I think I internalized the comical relief it brought to my family and ended up believing my art held no value. After that class, I do not remember painting again until recently in my life.

For this reason, I have decided to devote this chapter of my life to creativity. Writing, painting, dancing, and creating have helped bring me back to living a vibrant life. Shortly after beginning my writing journey, in the winter of 2021, I signed up to go on a trip abroad that following summer to Italy to learn and write poetry with Rachel Clift, known in the poetry world as R. Clift. She is an amazing poet, dear friend, and now mentor. When I came across her on Instagram, I instantly felt a deep resonance with her words and how she connected with her readers. Something in my whole body told me to go, to meet Rachel, and to invest in myself as an artist and writer.

This trip was one of the first times in my life I felt completely seen and safe to be the fullest expression of myself as a creative person. On the trip, we traveled from Rome to Florence to see the statue David, made pasta in a castle in Tuscany, got caught in a thunderstorm while dancing and singing to Whitney Huston's *I Want to Dance with Somebody* on top of Montecatini Alto on the most kismet last night of our retreat. And on that trip, the book of poetry you are currently holding in your hands flooded my body as I burst into tears holding a deep knowing that I was an artist and a writer. I told Rachel about this book and the vision I had to tell my story in an artistic way so that it could be shared with others. One year later, my book is ready to be birthed and set free into the world and fly on the wings of my unleashed creativity.

I used to think I could only create when I wasn't in school, but now, looking back, I can see how I have *always* been creating. As a professor, I have developed all of my own learning materials, lectures, and assignments mostly from scratch. I have created my business, *Inward Athlete*, creating content every day to remind athletes of the truth of who they are as a leader underneath any label. But most importantly, I write every single day and express myself through my poetry. I have so many ideas to put into the world that it can sometimes be overwhelming to think about how I am going to accomplish them all. I want to help shift others back home to themselves through my creative projects, mentorship, and ultimately, connect artists and dreamers back to their own life-force creative energy.

I want to create every single day until I can't create anymore.

I do not create to be perfect.

I create to be messy.

I create to get my ideas out of my head and into the world to add more love to the Earthly plane.

I believe it was reconnecting back to my creativity that saved my life.

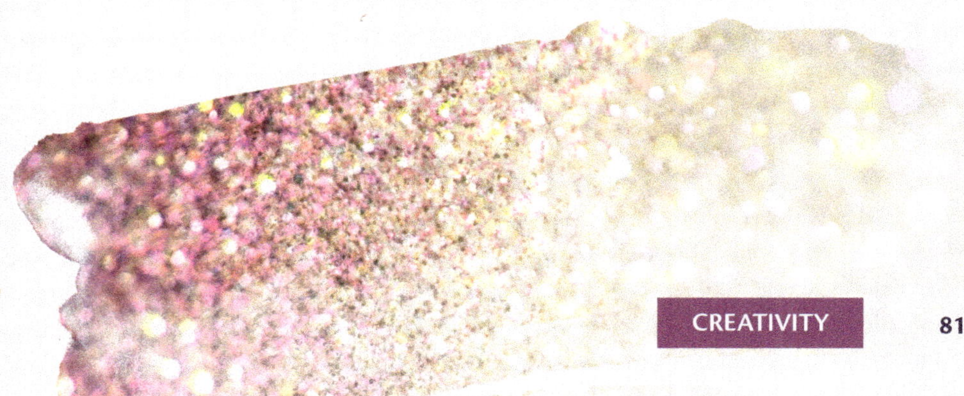

SHE DISSOLVED
INTO THE EARTH
AS LABELS THAT ONCE
DEFINED HER
BURNED INTO THE DIRT

CONSUMED BY THE
VOLCANO
THAT LIVED DEEP
WITHIN HER HEART

HER TRUE SELF
KEPT DORMANT
FOR FAR TOO LONG

FINALLY ERUPTING
UP TO THE SURFACE
AS HER WHOLE LIFE BECAME
TRANSFORMED BY THE LAVA

THEY WATCHED
AS SHE ROSE LIKE A PHOENIX
FROM THE ASHES
OF WHO SHE ONCE WAS

UNRECOGNIZABLE
TO THOSE WHO
ONCE KNEW HER
BACK FROM THE DEAD
STANDING TALL

IN HER

DIVINE

FEMININE

POWER

   HALF OF ME

what you would do

if you didn't need
to be doing anything

is probably what
you are meant
to be doing

I thought I lost you

And today
I was reminded
that you were indeed
never lost

Only just forgotten

Stowed away to collect dust
with the rest of my
childhood belongings

You waited patiently for me
for twenty years

Twenty years
of misplaced joy

Twenty years
of stagnant play

Twenty years
of creativity
waiting
to be unleashed

I'm glad I danced today

To remember I never lost you

I had only just forgotten you

"When I was thirteen,
my parents asked me
to choose between participating
in competitive dance or sports.
I chose sports.
I often wonder what my life
might have looked like today
if I had chosen dance.
In 2022, during my healing,
I went to an adult community
dance class and it inspired me
to write this poem.
The class reconnected me
back home to remember
my creative energy and
the childlike joy I had
in my creative energy
growing up."

After I pour my heart out
into the world
I'll pull back
to retreat into silence

Seeing clearly
for the first time
in a while
I will find

Enough sand
to build sand castles
inside my 2006
Chevy Cobalt

A home
where art
has exploded
all over
the walls

Sticky notes
full of dreams
and ideas
climbing
the windows

Books stacked disorderly
in every corner
of every room

Red lipstick
smeared across
the bathroom mirror

Fashion statements
spewed all over
the floorboards

Symbols of velvet armor
from fighting
the prior week's battle

Kitchen appliances
scattered across
the counter

Unwashed dishes
and utensils
piled inside the sink

Music blasting
on shuffle
covering
every
single
genre

And a collection
of salty tears
overflowing
the bathtub

And sometimes
when I find
a rare moment
caught inside
the eye of the storm

On peaceful nights
after the sun sets
and the stars come out
under the new moon

I wade in the stillness
to clean up the mess
I have made

But when I awake again
in the morning
and the sun shines
through my curtains
an all too familiar
alarm clock
reminds me

I am a hurricane

I wrote this poem on September 23rd, 2022, the week Hurricane Ian made landfall in Florida. As I looked around my apartment, I found myself in awe of the cleanliness of my space as I wrote. I love how storms clear the static of energy from the outside world and can bring the world into stillness.

Jen

YOU DEEPLY YEARN FOR THEM TO KNOW YOU

but you forget

HOW NOBODY COULD EVER UNDERSTAND

THE INNER WORLD OF A CREATIVE

He asked her
what does it feel like
when you're in your creative flow?

She proclaimed
it's a river
running down a mountainside
on its way to gush back out
into the ocean

It's electricity
coursing through my veins
charging up every cell
of my being

It's catching magnetic eyes
from a stranger
across the room
then seconds later
feeling the arrow of cupid
piercing me straight through my heart

It turns me on

It's love beaming through
every hardened layer
of my old decaying self

It's following a flicker of light
in the distance
guiding me straight to the foot
of a wildfire
burning through every corner
of my darkened past

It's bursting light bulbs on lampposts
one by one
as I drive down the highway
with my foot locked down
putting the pedal to the metal

It makes me feel fully alive

confetti kisses

I'm not sure
in my adult life
that I have ever had
a sober first kiss

I often wonder
what it must feel like

To be all the way alive

It must be like butterflies cracking their cocoons
for the very first time
I can feel them in my stomach
ready to take flight

Yet I have grown so used
to suppressing their flutter
mostly thinking it would be safer for them
to never leave the darkness

So I intentionally clip their wings
to keep them tame

Numbing the tingles
with too many drinks
it's casual anyways
nothing too serious
I become desensitized
so I can't feel a thing

Yet I often wonder
what it must feel like

To be all the way alive

HALF OF ME

It must be like confetti
bursting from a cannon
I can feel the pressure building
as my heart begins pounding

Yet, I have grown so used
to suppressing the friction
of an impending heart explosion
mostly thinking it would be safer
for the confetti
to never see the party

So I intentionally never
pull the trigger

Numbing the tingles
with too many drinks
it's casual anyway
nothing too serious
I become desensitized
so I can't feel a thing

Yet, I often wonder
what it must feel like

To be all the way alive

It must be like sailing across the ocean
underneath a cotton candy sky
watching the wind paint
a picture perfect
sailor's delight

Yet I have grown so used
to suppressing the magic
of a sunset
mostly thinking it would be safer
for me to never sail past dusk

So I intentionally never step foot
off the dry dock

Numbing the tingles
with too many drinks
it's casual anyways
nothing too serious
I become desensitized
so I can't feel a thing

Yet I often wonder what
it must feel like

To be all the way alive

I often think

*That's what a sober first kiss
must be like*

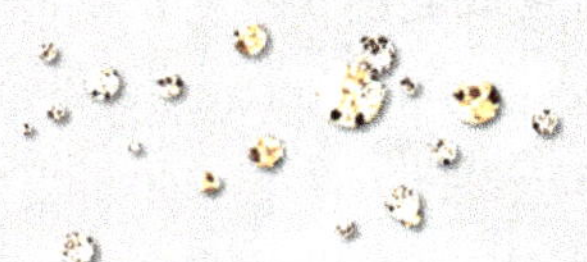

HALF OF ME

"Since the summer of 2020,
I have been living what I like to call
a sober-curious lifestyle.
I used to use alcohol to numb
my emotions and ease my nerves
to fit in at social events.
(I am actually more nervous
of the day when I get
my sober first kiss
than I am of you
reading this poem.)"

SHE CAME BACK HOME
TO HER HEART

AND FROM THAT PLACE
HER ART
BEGAN
TO
FLOW

AND WHEN HER ART
BEGAN
TO
FLOW

IT UNLOCKED THE PATH
FOR HER TO WALK FORWARD
INTO HER DIVINE MISSION

She has always known

That I was going to be valued
for my creativity

At the age of twenty-six
she bought me a six-string
electric guitar
forced me to borrow
her Ukelele
she said
I think you need a new hobby
and I still haven't learned
how to play either

She always told me
you know?
you could be just like Taylor Swift
if you wanted to

Both of us just unsure of how
to nurture my talents
maybe both of us afraid
of the reality of it

Still thinking
you still need health insurance
and a 401k
so don't go becoming Taylor Swift
too fast on us okay?

Until one day
we both saw
me again

HALF OF ME

Now healed
and in my element
sharing my medicine
through words
delivering my poetry
out to the masses

I find it funny today
that the only instrument
I ever needed was a pen

Today people listening
to my words
confirm it

Just like one man told me
you're the Taylor Swift of poets

So be careful
I'll write you
in and out
of my life
With every stroke
of my pen
And turning
of a page

My mother has always known it

at the core of every
over-committed

dedicated

and strong-willed
perfectionist

is an artist

of a once

carefree

creative child

WHAT MEMORIES DO YOU HAVE OF YOURSELF IN CREATIVE PLAY AS A CHILD?

In these memories is where your magic hides

I wish you could see yourself
through my eyes

Because what I see
is a rainbow casting colors
across the sky
exploding with dynamite
up into the Heavens

Honoring the remembrance
of how your soul came here
on a mission
flying across the galaxies
just for the chance
to make it Earth-side

With a beating human heart
full of love to give
just wanting to be witnessed

Planting your seeds
of the tallest redwood trees
rooting yourself into the Earth
to be seen by all the future generations
gifting them with a walk
through your magic forest
of potential

My dear

I want to assist you to become
the highest version of you
and to see yourself
in the light I see you

HALF OF ME

SHE TAKES HERSELF ON ARTIST DATES
SPENDING TIME IN THE FREEDOM
OF UNPLANNED MAGIC

HOLDING ONTO THE VISIONS
OF HER FUTURE

SITTING WITH HER HEART
LISTENING TO ITS KNOWING

TUNING INTO WHAT'S READY
TO BE SHARED WITH THE WORLD

BECAUSE SHE KNOWS
EVERYTHING IS ALL HAPPENING NOW

SO SHE SPENDS HER TIME
IN THE FREEDOM OF UNPLANNED MAGIC
TO DRAW THE FUTURE TOWARDS HER

"you are here
to share
your heart's
desires
with the
world"

WHAT DID YOUR SOUL COME HERE TO CREATE IN THIS LIFETIME?

part iv.

Connection

We are biologically hardwired as humans for social connection. For this reason, we often exhibit behaviors in our lives that will fill our need for belonging. Most of my life, I was always trying to gain the approval of others to meet this need. I perceived love by how quickly I could perform a task for someone else and be validated to get work done— just like I had with sports. I held onto sports for so long because that is where I found community.

When I was thirteen, my dad asked me to choose between competitive dance or sports. It was getting too expensive for me to continue participating in both. I can't remember the process I went through to make the decision, or if I was ever guided by one by my parents, but I ended up choosing my love for basketball, soccer, softball, and volleyball. Looking back now, I believe I chose sports because that is how I perceived receiving love from my family and friends most of my life. Playing sports was how I connected to others. I never remember my parents missing a game of mine growing up as a child and as a three-sport athlete in high school. One time, my dad even sat in the bleachers of an away volleyball match as he was passing a kidney stone (bless his heart). We spent countless hours of quality time on car rides to tournaments and practices. My sports teams were like my extended family. No matter what, through the wins and losses, I always had people in my life who wouldn't abandon me. I chose sports because of the safety, connection, and love they brought into my life.

I held onto my sports identity for as long as I could. I worked various jobs in college athletics and studied topics on how people could feel more connected to themselves and others. When I began to relinquish the need to feel fulfilled through my "team" identity I began to connect back to myself again. I also lost myself in men to try to feel connected.

Most of my twenties I used men and the urgent need to find romantic partnership to feel fulfilled. The last time I called someone a boyfriend was in college. He cheated on me with his ex-girlfriend. I found out by reading a sticky note posted on his bathroom mirror— not in my handwriting— that read, "I will always love you Nick - love Ashley." After that relationship, I continued a loop in unhealthy patterns with men. I was starving for connection and to feel loved and validated through intimate romantic partnership. Operating from my conditioning the pat-

    HALF OF ME

tern went; *find a man, sleep with him, and that will make him love me.* Now, becoming consciously aware of this pattern, I have realized in order to cultivate a high value, worthy relationship with another person (romantic or platonic) one must act from a place of high self worth and value within themselves first and foremost. I have taken the last two years to cultivate a healthy connection with myself so that I can now build healthy relationships with others.

Today, I am still learning how to set intentional boundaries with others and source my love from within. These days, I choose to not measure my love and validation from the praise I receive from others, or how quickly I can answer an email, or how fast I can grade a set of papers, or how well I can please a man in bed. I do what feels right to honor and love myself unconditionally. I set time-limits around my work hours (which is still something I am navigating while transitioning into the life of an entre-preneur) and work to be mindful and present with myself and others no matter the situation.

And at the same time, I can now give myself grace during all of the times I was oper-ating from my conditioning, because there was a little girl inside me that just wanted to have her needs met and to be loved. What would it look like for you to source your love from within you first before you go grab the vice or exhibit the behavior that numbs your feelings of being alone? I want you to know that you are deserving of love right now in this current moment because you are whole and complete just as you are today.

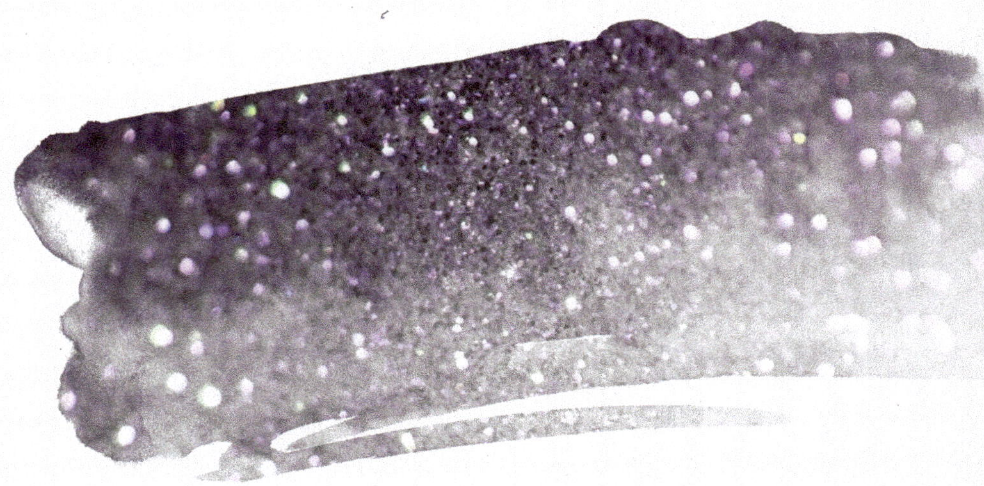

SHE WANDERS
AROUND THE WORLD

SEARCHING FOR THE ONES
WHO REMEMBER
WHO THEY ARE

SO THAT THEIR RESONANCE
OF TRUTH
WILL BRING HER BACK HOME
TO HERSELF

i looked for love
outside of myself

for so long

until i remembered

that the environment
outside of me

is just reflecting back at me

the love i hold

deep

inside

for myself

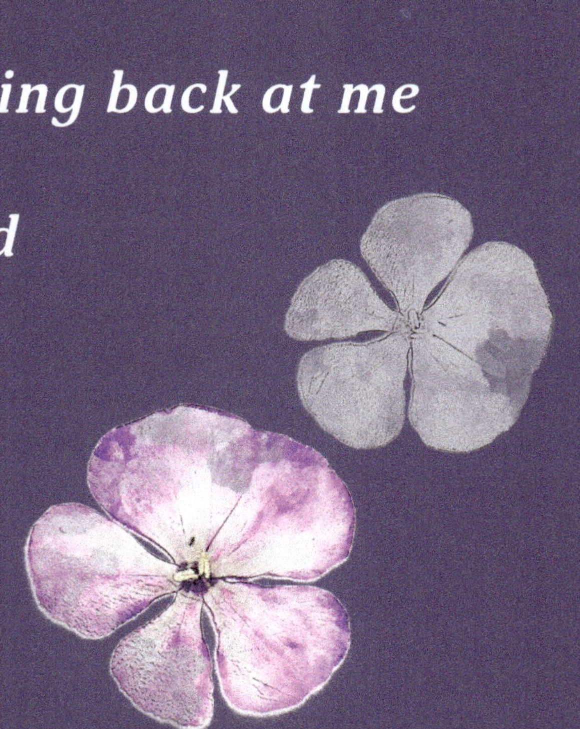

We don't say
I love you

Or do hugs
in my family

But my mom
gives the best gifts

My dad
makes the best food

My sister
holds us all together
with her candor

And I provide
the emotional
alchemy

Each one of us
shows I love you
in our own
special kind of way

So, I like to think
I love you

Can be expressed
in a million
different of ways

HALF OF ME

"On my journey of healing,
I had to heal my relationship
with the expectations of love
I desired to receive from others.
I have learned that the love we desire
is often the love we need
to give to ourselves.
Also, others can't read our minds.
So if you want to receive love
in a certain kind of way,
it takes courage to consciously
communicate your needs
with another person."

The last memory
I have of her touch
is her rubbing my back
as I slumbered off
to sleep

Age five

Then one night
It was done

Her fingernails
that once soothed
the length of
my spine

Nurtured hands
of a lullaby's touch

She was gone

No more bedtime stories
left to cradle me
in her arms
of sweet love

Just a goodnight

As she nodded off
to the TV
under her
dim lamp

With a library book
on her lap

She'd say
don't forget to turn off the kitchen lights
before going to bed

That's the last time
I remember her loving touch

I want her to know
I will always be
her little girl

I love you mom

hungry for comfort

Sometimes I make the decision
to binge eat a whole pizza
on a Friday night

And contrary
to what you
might think
it's a decision I make
from a place of self love
And to feel
a sense of safety

You see
the child within me
still holds tight
to the love I felt
when my dad and I
would drive downtown
to our local pizza parlor
almost every Friday night

Most times
we would sit in silence
and other times sing
to Air Supply

And the safety I felt
in that car
on Friday nights
is sometimes hard to replace
in my adult human life

I grew up as a child
watching my hardworking parents
hustle through the work week
just to have the chance
to relax on the weekend

And together as a family
we would find solace
around our kitchen table
bite by lovingly pizza bite

And today
it takes a conscious effort
to understand my heart

To examine why these old habits
truly do die hard

Because believe me

I do see
how these old habits
no longer serve
the highest version of me

But sometimes
on Friday nights
when the feeling of loneliness
comes knocking on my door

I pick-up my phone
and scroll through my apps
and send out an SOS
to good ole Papa John's pizza store

And as I place the order
I send up some loving prayers
to my younger self
I allow her to go there

Because in this conscious choice
I know
that my human self
just wants to feel safe

And in these moments
meditation
breathwork
and gentle walks
around my apartment complex
just won't suffice

And as I eat
bite by lovingly pizza bite

I remember the car rides
the silence
and the singing to Air Supply

And how the safety that was held
in that space
between my dad and I
is still stored there
in the very back of my mind

So
that's why
sometimes
I make the decision
to binge eat a whole pizza
on a Friday night

 HALF OF ME

WHAT ARE THE THINGS AND/OR BEHAVIORS IN YOUR LIFE THAT YOU USE TO NUMB THE FEELINGS OF LONELINESS IN ORDER TO FEEL MORE CONNECTED?

For me, it was food, alcohol, sex, binging TV, and gossip.

SHE SAID
TAKE YOUR TIME
WITH ME

SHOW UP DAILY
SO THAT YOU CAN LEARN
THE RESONANCE
OF EACH OF MY
GUITAR STRINGS

CHOOSE TO SLOWLY
STRUM THE CHORDS
OF MY HEART

SO THAT YOU
CAN HELP ME
PIECE BACK TOGETHER
THE SONG
OF
MY
SOUL

HALF OF ME

There is shame
woven in my secrecy
hiding behind
my smiled lies

Year after year
I shrank
smaller
and
smaller

Each lie I told
built more remorse
around my breaking heart

A guilty conscious
rising in a child
yearning to become a woman

Wanting to explore
and experience
my wild

Do anything
to feel
the safe loving touch
of another

Yet ringing in my ears
was the voice
of my mother

*Don't you ever forget
no way's the only way*

So I ripped off
my chastity belt
in an act of rebellion

Confused
on how to get
any man to love me

Humiliated
one encounter
after another

Doing anything
to protect a smeared reputation
of their perfect daughter

You see
there is shame woven
in my secrecy
and therein lies
a beautiful truth

I cared more
about protecting them
from the image
I was becoming

Too shameful to share
with them the whole story
of my undoing

I know they would have saved me

If only I had felt
safe enough
to tell them the truth

MY MOST VULNERABLE POEM.

I want you to fuck me

Use me for your pleasure
claim me as your lover
and devour me with your eyes

Rock me
so when the earth quakes
beneath us
you leave me
in full body quivers

But woah woah woah

I should slow down

Before I get ahead of myself
I should have asked

Just what are your intentions
with my body?

Before I stand before you
and begin to strip down
all my layers?

I think we should set the stage right now
of what this could be

I mean
is it a one time
or a forever
kind of thing?

If there's one thing
I know for sure
I've learned that
masterful connections
are built on
hard-to-have conversations

And it's a paradox you know

Either I tell you all my needs
then you'll run to your boys
and call me a psycho
Or I lay down and we do it
and I shut my mouth
then I'm labeled a whore
and become the talk of the town

And I think you should know
I only ask from experience
because I've come to this crossroads
too many times before

I mean
I'm still mad at all the men
who were conditioned to believe
that they'd become king

if they were to sleep with me

leave me

then throw away the key

It's taken me too many years to understand
that no man of mine
would choose to just fuck me
then leave me

And each time in my past
I laid in a new bed
I gave away the most
vulnerable parts of myself
that took forever to get back

Oh and don't get me wrong
there were times
I used their bodies too

wrapped in my own type
of shameful dopamine cycles
just to feel my own
lustful surges on loop

And through all of this
I've just been playing out
the physical embodiment
of my abandoned inner child

But I digress

So us?

Are we stuck
in a throwback
teenage dream?

Or are we grown ass adults
ready for real intimacy?

And before you talk
can I just tell you a secret
I've never told any man before?

I'm probably not going to even enjoy it
unless I trust you're grounded in integrity
and are a safe place to run to

These days
I'd rather be turned on by your values
oh, you're a humanitarian?
tell me all about it

And I don't want to meet you at this bar
I want to meet you in real life
living out your mission
cranking out your business plan
typing away at your vision

And when we pass each other
by on the street
and we catch each other's stares
I'll find you speaking truth
into lost souls on the sidewalk
directing them on a path
back home to themselves

Now
that's the man
I want to fuck

So, if that's you
please

Use me for your pleasure
claim me as your lover
and devour me with your eyes

Rock me
so when the earth quakes
beneath us
you leave me
in full body quivers

I wrote this poem after hearing Maureen McDole, a poet in St. Pete, FL, perform at one of the first open mics I ever attended. The first line of her poem, I Want You to Fuck Me, activated emotions in me in such a way that I went home that night to try and write an erotic poem. The poem above ended up taking me on an unexpected healing journey that I didn't know I needed.

Jen

*the only skeletons
in my closet*

*are all the men
i tried to love*

*thinking they would
come back to life*

*with a beating heart
to love me*

They say
I'll find you
when neither of us
are looking

Yet, how can I not look for you
when I've already met you?

I've already felt your presence here
in this home I've been building

In my dreams
dancing with me
through my meditations

I've smelt the coals of the fire on you
that you've kept burning

At the beach
where we'll build our future home
upon the shores together

I've felt your hand
clasped in mine
as we laid on our backs
gazing up at the stars

Telling each other stories
of how long it took
to reunite back together
in this lifetime

Those who say
I'll find you
when neither of us
are looking

HALF OF ME

*Must not know
what it's like
to have already met
their person*

They must not know
what it's like
to have already connected
to their perfect partner's
soul's essence

Jen

I spent countless years
looking into fogged-up mirrors
smeared smudges
wiped across the glass
as blurry reflections of myself
were the only ones
I ever saw
mirrored back

Until one day
you showed up
holding a brand new mirror

One free of scratches
or greasy fingerprints
you stood fearlessly steady
as you held it up

And what I saw
when I lifted my eyes
to meet my own gaze
was a crystal clear vision
of new kind of woman
and for the first time ever
I was ready to be seen

As I lost myself in your humble presence
you invited me to step forward
and join you
on the other side of the mirror

Just as Alice did
stepping through the looking glass
the higher version of myself
decided to enter into Wonderland

Then all of a sudden
a whole new reality emerged
one built on love
and the truth of God

   HALF OF ME

Now standing side by side
I followed you back
towards a sovereign light

And as we walked
the path eventually came to an end
where we stopped
and took a silent pause

Then in that moment
you handed the mirror back to me

As we parted ways
I held tight to my new mirror
now newly minted with your magic
that you infused in its reflection

I decided on that day
to never put it down
embedded with the wisdom
you taught me

I'd begin on a whole new journey
holding it up
and reflecting
it back to others

This poem is dedicated to my mentors, Dr. Brendan Dwyer, Dr. Carrie LeCrom, Dr. Greg Greenhalgh, and Aaron Rose.

Jen

WHO ARE THE PEOPLE IN YOUR LIFE WHO HAVE SEEN THINGS IN YOU THAT YOU COULDN'T YET SEE FOR YOURSELF AND WHAT ARE THE QUALITIES THEY MIRRORED BACK TO YOU?

SHE DECIDED ONE DAY
SHE WAS WORTH AN INNER CIRCLE
OF LOYAL CONSCIOUS CREATORS

A CHOSEN FAMILY
THAT VIBRATE WITH THE RISE
AND FALL OF THE SUN

ONES WHO UPLIFT HER
INTO THE WOMAN
OF WHO SHE'S BECOMING

LEAVING BEHIND
THE ONES
WHO NO LONGER GET HER

SHE UNDERSTANDS
HER VIBRATIONAL RESONANCE
WILL REARRANGE HER PEOPLE

WHILE SOME
WILL FALL AWAY
NEW ONES WILL INEVITABLY
FALL INTO PLACE

Those are my people

The ones who risk
all that others have known them to be
so they can be known
for just who they are
in the truest essence
of their soul

The ones who are brave enough
to be witnessed
for all of their colors

The ones who slowly peel back
each of their layers
in a mysterious fashion

Slow enough to keep you wondering
yet fast enough
to draw you in

The ones who are unafraid
to express themselves
in their raw emotion

The ones who jump
and spread their wings to fly
before ever searching
for the safety net beneath them

The ones who hold sacred space
with a listening ear
because they have sat
in the depths
of their own silence
and know the healing power
of boundless time

My people take you with them
on their journey

so you can learn from their
triumphs and
their failures

My people
don't hold back

Their hearts

Or their tears

Or their laughter

And in their expression
grant you permission
to do the same

They are the ones
who flow in rhythm
with the crest of the Earth
that vibrates beneath their feet

*They are the ones casting visions
of hope fought for
on the battlefields
of their own
war torn hearts*

They are the ones
with their feet on the ground
and their spirits flying
towards the light

That's how my people
pave a path out of the darkness
from which they themselves
have emerged from

So that others don't have to
face their shadows alone

Those are my people

"I have learned that the standards
we have for ourselves is what
we will attract into our lives
as standards in others.
In other words, embody the values
and characteristics of the people
you want to be surrounded with
and they will come.
And once these people start coming,
hold them closely, and let them know
how much they inspire you.
You will notice, they will reflect
the same back at you."

To the man
who wants to try and love me

I am reckless

I have broken more than just glass
in this lifetime

Sometimes I move too fast
and get carried away
with the wind

Just like that one time
I almost sank my whole family
on a pontoon boat ride
submerging us
by shifting into full throttle
a little bit too fast

Or the other time
I put all the skins of the veggies
from my juicer
down my brother-in-law's
garbage disposal
and I burned out the motor

I've also broken hearts

I can be lazy
as I wait patiently
for my creative urges
to build up inside me
so that I can unleash them
all at once

I often wait around
wandering
from place to place
seeking inspiration

And what may appear
to be making
no progress forward

I promise you my
brain is always working

And that this art
that I hold in my heart
will eventually come out
if I let it build long enough

I believe it will shift the world
for the better
so I continue to wait
and I know that looks lazy

I am an over-thinker
and while I'm better
than I've ever been before
I can sometimes get caught up
in all the stories
of a future fairytale ending
that only lives in my head
or in other dimensions

And I may or may not
get carried away thinking
one day it will be you
who will get down on one knee
confessing your undying love for me

And then on the day after you do
there's a story I create
that believes you may choose
to then just get up and leave me

   HALF OF ME

I am a spiritual seeker
and not to get too woo-woo on you
but I'm pretty sure I'm a witch
and a psychic
and an intuitive knower
feeling my way
through this energetic plane
of all of existence

Talking to my ancestors
through my pen
and manifesting
through my spoken prayers

I am a healer

And I bring medicine to others
by just standing firm
in my own truth

But most importantly
I'm a lover
and my heart is more wide-open
than it's ever been before

So I just thought I would warn you
before you try to love me
I am reckless

WHAT ARE THE THINGS IN THE WAY BLOCKING YOUR CONNECTION TO COMING BACK HOME TO YOUR SELF?

(Self = higher self/spirit/internal guidance system)

HALF OF ME

part v.

Surrender

I stood there, in a darkened United Methodist Church as the congregation stood around the pews making a circle on the outside of the sanctuary. One person started with a lighted wax candle, and then, one by one, each person passed the flame from their candle onto the next until the entire congregation's fire lit the church with a soft white light and everyone began to sing *Silent Night*. It's 2000, Christmas Eve, and I can feel Christ's love all around me, moving through each chain reaction of light passing from one person to the next. It is still one of my favorite days of the year to go to church, because it is one of the only days of the year I can actually *feel* the spirit of God move through every single person who came to worship through song, their light, and the common intention to bless a savior.

Growing up, I never resonated with being told what to believe. I only know what it feels like to be connected to something greater outside of myself. Because most Sundays did not allow me to feel connected to the emotion of love, I stopped going to church when I left my hometown for college.

In my twenties, I was searching desperately for the same feeling I had on Christmas Eves growing up. I wouldn't begin to reconnect back to my spirituality until 2018. That year, I found myself in my spare time during graduate school sitting in my living room, watching Oprah's Super Soul Sunday on T.V. While I watched, I took notes in my notebook dedicated to understanding spiritual teachers' definitions of God, love, and the soul. That year I put Oprah's book *The Wisdom of Sundays: Life-Changing Insights from Super Soul Conversations* on my Christmas wish list to dive deeper into these teachings. My logical mind wanted to believe it all to be true, and I wanted these spiritual teachers to show me the way to find a God I still could not yet feel.

One year later, I sat in my bedroom hunched over on my knees as I labeled myself agnostic. I still could not feel anything connecting me to a higher power. That summer, God would come thundering back into my life as I laid there on the hot pavement wrapped in the Alabama heat as I prayed for God for the first time to relieve my burdens. I closed my eyes and almost instantly felt the heavy weight I had been carrying get lifted off my chest. After that experience, I began to journal every day to try to understand the connection I had felt. That year, I deeply yearned to build a consistent and intimate connection with God/Universe/Source/Spirit (GUSS).

Two years later, after writing every day, I sought refuge in a mentor named Aaron Rose, a spiritual teacher and transformational coach, who has a course called *God Is*

My Boss. I was fortunate to get to work with him one-on-one to consciously build my business Inward Athlete. He invited me into a deeper practice with God and encouraged me to begin each day with a new ritual by having *a morning meeting with God*. So each morning since working with him, I have surrendered *my will to thy will* and have prayed to be guided in my mission each and every day.

After one of my first one-on-one sessions with Aaron, I began to integrate a prayer of surrender into my morning daily practice. I began to feel a daily and consistent force of love again move through me which began to weave throughout every moment of my daily life. One time, I had such a profound meditation where I was lifted out of my body, seeing an image of myself being cradled by the energy of God, comforted, and then laid back down into my body.

If you do not know who, what, or if a God outside of you exists, or what the energy of creation is, I invite you to begin to ask to feel its presence of God move in your life. Get still and connect to the force of energy and love all around you in the present moment.

For myself, I had to remove a lot of limiting beliefs and behaviors that were rooted in believing that I was unworthy to receive a love that was all-consuming and unconditional. I had to remove a lot of stored emotions built up in my physical body and trade suppressing my emotions for expressing them. I had to remove alcohol and other forms of coping mechanisms and trade happy hours for my creative outlets. I had to remove my mistrust in a higher power and throw complete faith into a feeling and begin to cultivate a new relationship with the feeling of God in my life. Once I started, everything began to change.

A PRAYER FOR SURRENDER

SHE SUBMITTED HERSELF
TO A GREATER PLAN
SHE COULD NOT YET SEE

SHE CHOSE NOT TO
WRITE THE ENDING
OF HER STORY
BEFORE IT EVEN BEGAN

SHE PUT HER HANDS UP
AND LET GOD GRAB HER WRISTS

THEN ASKED TO BE GUIDED
ON HER DIVINE PATH AHEAD

*it will be hard to
leave behind*

*everything you thought
you wanted*

and at the same time

you know

*it would be even harder
to stay*

I don't want to be a poet

I don't want to have to quit
my stable day job
just to afford myself the freedom
to feel the whole spectrum
of every human emotion
more deeply

I don't want to be a poet

Or the black sheep
of my family
any longer

I've already lived my whole life
wandering this sheep pasture
roaming around desperately
trying to fit in with a family
who just thinks I'm crazy

I no longer want to hold
all of these pieces
from all of these places
stored in my heart
that have long ago expired

They are getting heavy
and sometimes
I think
I can't bare to hold them
any longer

HALF OF ME

And while you may witness me
as a vision of peace
the only way
for me to get to this place
was to fight through
all of the pressure
so that I could find myself
caught inside the calm
of the eye of the storm
all too well knowing
the storm has to pass back
through me again
with all the same elements
that tossed me around
the first time

I never asked to live a life
that brings me to my knees
asking for reprieve
from all these heavy feelings
that I can only alchemize

With the swift strokes of my pen

or my breath

or deep moments of solitude
filled with silence

I don't want to be a poet

And I've tried all these years

to become everything
other than the starving artist archetype
until I realized
that's the only way
my soul knows how to be

I don't want to be a poet

And I never asked to save myself
with just these words
but that's exactly who
I came here to be
just now remembering

So maybe

If I choose to be a poet
I can be all the things
and do all the things
I've been avoiding to be
for the past thirty-three years

HALF OF ME

"This poem was inspired
by poet and friend, Marques Clark.
His poem titled, *A Poet's Poem*,
struck a healing chord within me
the first time I heard him read it.
It allowed me to surrender further
into my artistry. It helped me
begin to claim my title as a poet
and it has been one of the wildest,
most beautiful journeys of my life
ever since."

WHAT ARE THINGS IN YOUR LIFE YOU REALLY WANT TO BE DOING BUT DO NOT BELIEVE THEY ARE REALISTIC FOR YOU TO BE DOING?

I grew sharp edges
around my heart
wielding unknowing knives
into the backs of others

Slicing those who might get too close

Untouchable
therefore
unlovable

But, even *Edward Scissorhands*
was deeply loved
for just who he was

So I remember
how my hard exterior
is no match
to letting down my guard

To be seen
for all I was created to be
my sharp edges and all

Growing up, I remember renting *Edward Scissorhands* from our local library every week
for a stretch of time. I think I must have resonated with the storyline of being the outcast
and different even as a young child. I also think it's weird my mom let me binge watch this
movie as a child.

Jen

HALF OF ME

I know what it's like
to romanticize
leaving this Earthly plane

And in the same breath
I remember
how my spirit
came here to create

And to cut my life short
would not only be a disservice to me
but a disservice
to humanity

Because if I left

I wouldn't get to tell my story

And others
wouldn't get to see
the world
through my eyes

"I have never had a plan
to commit suicide, but I have
romanticized how it sometimes
might be easier to just let it all go
and dissolve myself from this
physical plane of existence. If you
or someone you know needs
immediate support right now,
you can call the Suicide and
Crisis Lifeline at 988.
There are infinite possibilities of who you
can become, what you can do,
and where you can go in this lifetime.
We need you here to step
into these possibilities and bring
more love to this Earthly plane."

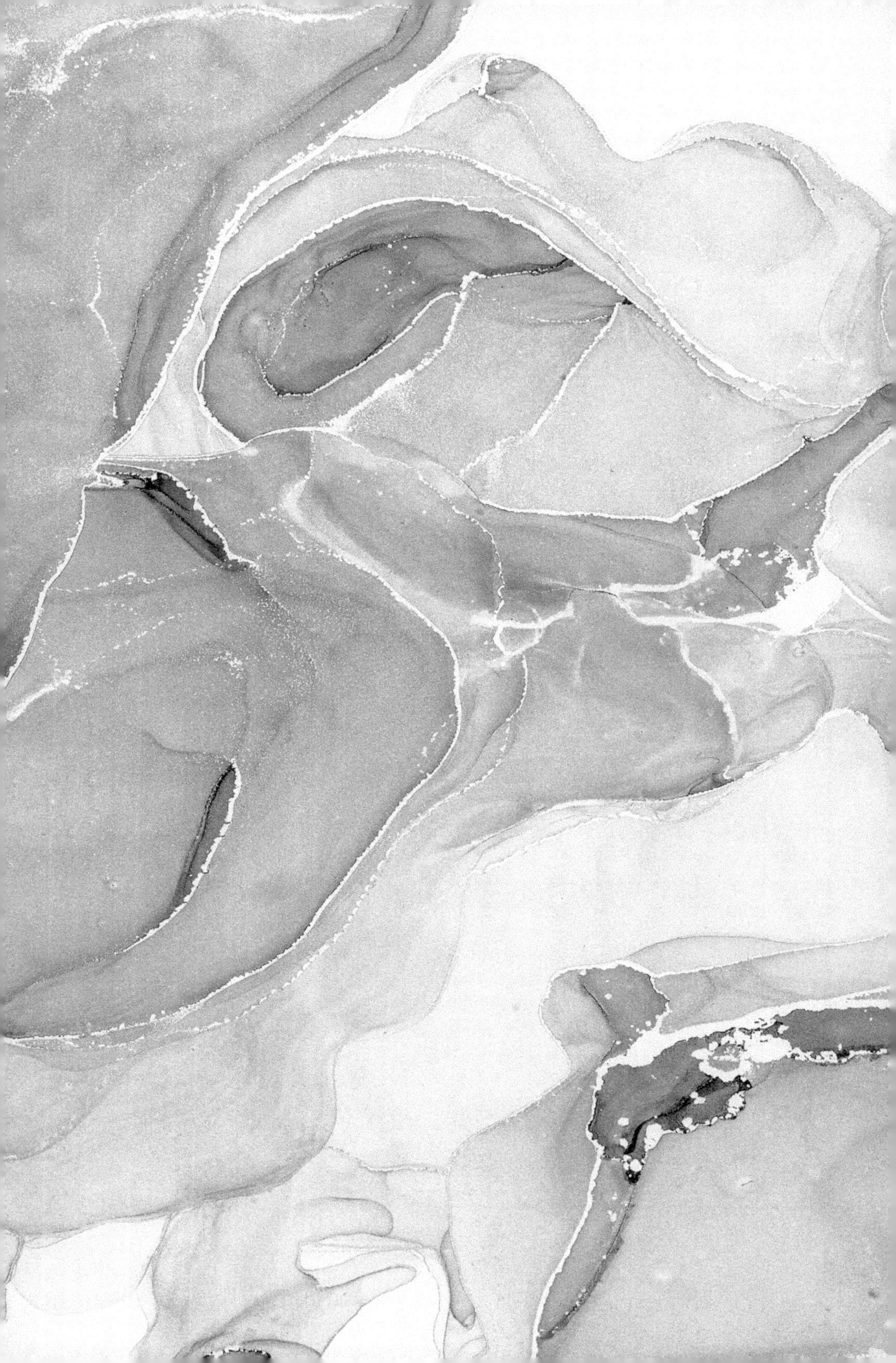

JUST WHEN SHE THOUGHT
SHE MIGHT DROWN
SHE CAME KICKING FURIOUSLY
BACK UP TOWARDS THE SURFACE

GASPING FOR BREATH
AS SHE SUCKED IN THE AIR
ABOVE THE THE WATER
TO STAY ALIVE

INHALING DEEPLY
AND SOAKING IN
THE BEAUTY ALL AROUND HER

IT WAS ONLY THEN SHE REALIZED
IT WAS TIME TO BUILD A LIFE
OUTSIDE THE OCEAN

SO NOW
EACH AND EVERYDAY
THAT'S WHERE SHE BEGINS

KICKING HERSELF BACK UP
TOWARDS THE LIGHT OF DAY

With just one subtle touch of another
I will surely crumble

Just as sandcastles
dissolve in the wind
grain by grain
blown away
into the abyss

A crack in the windshield
ready to spiderweb
into every corner of the glass
that is my life

Raw to each syllable
of every spoken word
of another

Their voices prick me

Get stuck inside me

Like the pin cushion
my mother uses
to stow away
her sewing needles

On the verge
of a waterfall moment
right here
in front of
all these strangers

So I suck back my tears
into my eyeballs
damming up the potential river
that could surly take out an entire city

An inevitable flood
that is about to sweep
away my heart

But in that moment
I take a breath
and decide to let it flow

Where I used to hold it in
I have learned to let it go

Because I know now
that when the rain dries
and the sun comes out again
I will be reborn

As a sensitive soul and empathic human, this is what it can feel like to think about being hugged when I am at the height of my emotions.

Jen

SHE STANDS ON THE SHORELINE
WAVING HER WHITE FLAG
TOWARDS THE WATER

ONE LAST ATTEMPT
AT A FAITHFUL SURRENDER

GIVING HERSELF OVER
TO A FORCE
MUCH MORE POWERFUL
THAN HER

YOU SEE
*SHE HAS FOUGHT AGAINST THE CURRENT
FOR TOO LONG*

A SEA THAT ONCE CHURNED HER
IN CIRCLES
OF THE STORIES
SHE ONCE TOLD HERSELF

BUT HERE TODAY
WHERE THE WATER
MEETS THE SAND
SHE FEELS FREE
FOR THE FIRST TIME
IN HER LIFE

SO SHE LET HERSELF GO
AND WADED
INTO THE THE TIDES
TRUSTING THEY WILL CARRY HER
WHEREVER SHE IS MEANT TO GO

What if we chose
not to judge the presence
of our sadness?

Could you imagine?

To never cast
grief as the villain

Shame
sorrow's existence

Sever melancholy
from our hearts

Shove regret aside
until happiness comes along

What if

Like us

It all just wants
to be noticed?

Can't you remember
what it felt like?

When they cast you aside
as the villain?

Shamed you for
your existence?

Severed you from
their heart?

And shoved you aside
until something better came along?

We are the same
as our sadness

Both of us

Wanting to be uplifted
witnessed
and welcomed home
into the open arms
of unconditional love

You were made of love
from the center
of the universe

Birthed from
its fiery core
encased inside
a clear rose quartz

Friction of love
molding you
as a child of God

Delivered through
the dark portal
of your mother's womb

Finding your way
staggering onto
this Earth

But quickly
after arriving
the purity of your heart
was stripped year after year
by societal programming

Residue of fear
hate and jealousy
stuck inside you
blocking the way
for infinite
intimate connection

Until the day
you began to learn how
to love yourself again
so that the energy
could restore
your body

   HALF OF ME

To come home
into resonance
with your spirit
and have the courage
to remember

Just who the fuck you are

Poetry has already brought so many amazing people into my life. This poem was written in a small group, hosted by my dear friend and poet Oksanna Normandeau, and a writing prompt she offered us to begin with the first line,
"I was made from the center of the universe."

Jen

SHE SAT THERE THINKING
HOW *BEING*
IS PROBABLY THE MOST IMPORTANT THING
US HUMANS COULD BE DOING

AS SHE FELT THE CHAOS
OF THE OUTSIDE WORLD
SPIN AROUND HER
SHE DECIDED TO COME
BACK HOME
TO THE CORE OF HER ESSENCE
AND LET IT
RESTORE HER BODY

TO JUST BE
AND LET THE BEING
RECALIBRATE HER HEART

WHAT A POWERFUL DECLARATION IT WAS
TO NO LONGER SUBSCRIBE
TO A CULTURE OF HUSTLE
THAT HAS BUILT A SYSTEM
OF DETACHED HUMANS
CUT OFF FROM THEIR SPIRITS
LONG ENOUGH
TO CONTROL THE NARRATIVE
OF WHAT'S RIGHT
AND WHAT'S WRONG

SHE KNOWS
OUR INTERNAL COMPASSES
HAVE ALWAYS HELD THE TRUTH
AND THEY LIVE
WITHIN EACH OF US

SHE SAT THERE THINKING
HOW SHE SHOULD JUST CONTINUE BEING

 HALF OF ME

one day
you will rise
before the rest
of the world does

and in the
stillness

you will
remember
why you came

WHAT ARE YOU AFRAID OF?

My favorite journaling prompt.

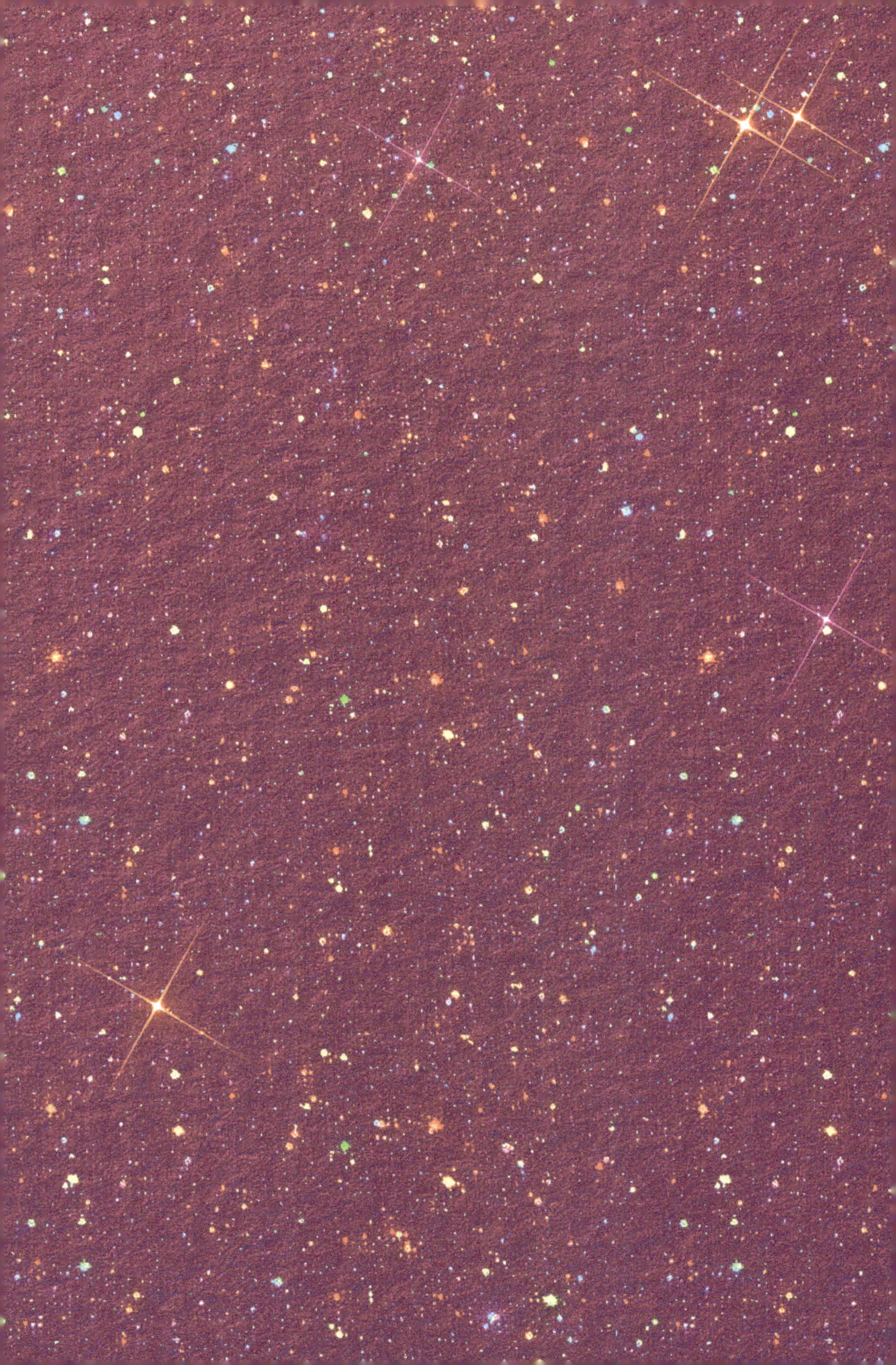

part vi.

Trust

With tears in my eyes, I looked down at the red marks and a big "C" scribbled across the top of my very first college essay. "What can I do better?" I asked the professor as tears streamed down my face. He looked up at me with pity in his eyes, as he must have been thinking, *how did you get here, and who taught you how not to write?*

It was freshman year of college and I was in my first year writing class. Up to that point, my English teachers had only taught me how to write the five paragraph essay. I became very good at the algorithm: introduce to the writer your topic, drop three paragraphs of facts, and then write a concluding paragraph. I was the best five-paragraph essay writer you would ever meet. I was good at learning the rules to meet the requirements of the educational system. When my professor told me an essay could have more than five paragraphs, someone could have probably picked my jaw up off the floor. I was shocked. I believe that man only let me through class with an "A" because of my work ethic to try to undo my conditioning of the five paragraph essay, not because I was a good writer. After that class, I chose to major in Physical Education to stay as far away from writing as possible.

In my first semester of graduate school as a Doctoral Student, I was asked to write a paper on why I was getting my Ph.D. and to present the research topics I was most interested in. I went to my professor's office who was an English Ph.D. and I told her I could not write. I was stuck and nothing would come out. Tears began to stream down my face as I felt broken, inadequate, and like an imposture for being in a program that required me to one day write a whole dissertation. She looked up at me with pity in her eyes and must have been thinking, *how did you get here, and who taught you how not to write?* For many years, I let my shame lead me into days of self-loathing and procrastination because I felt unqualified to be a writer of any kind.

I was embarrassed, but that teacher planted a seed in me that serves me to this day. She told me to write in a stream of consciousness. She encouraged me to "write about anything and whatever comes to mind." I would not actually use this advice until after my Ph.D. was complete, but it is a tool I use today to process my emotions when feelings of inadequacy arise to the surface. I am able to move through my emotions and then move into a flow that sparks my creativity. When I have energy that feels stuck inside me I write to undo the limiting beliefs that are holding me back and then rewrite new ones.

  HALF OF ME

My past self would never believe where I am today, as I proudly call myself a writer and a poet. In the summer of 2020, when I began to examine the resistance in my life that I was facing, I began to journal about all of the things I was currently feeling and experiencing in my life. Then I began to write about all of the things I truly desired, who I truly believed myself to be, and what I truly wanted to feel and manifest in my future. Writing it all down has been a powerful practice in my life and something that feels like Source flowing directly through my pen. Once I began journaling and writing in an unrestricted way, with no rules, or obligations, or pressure, was the day I became a writer.

To this day, I have never been trained how to be a "good" writer, and that makes me feel like the biggest imposture at times. I do not know proper grammar, or how to structure a perfect sentence, but I do know my emotions and the feelings that flow through my pen when I write them on a page or speak to a group of listeners or on nights I attend open mics to read my words. For someone to resonate with my words, feels like the deepest honor and truth my body has ever known. Without even knowing it, writing has been a thread throughout my whole life. I will continue to trust in the unseen path ahead. I have no idea where my writing will take me but it is something I must continue doing because it feels like what I am meant to be doing, and I trust in that.

SHE CHANGED HER LIFE
BY SHIFTING INTO
THE FUTURE VERSION
OF WHO SHE ENVISIONED
HERSELF TO BE

OVER AND
OVER AGAIN
MAKING SMALL PIVOTS
INTO HERSELF
SLOWLY

FOLDING EACH
NEW INGREDIENT
INTO A NEW IDENTITY

PEACE

CREATIVITY

CONNECTION

FREEDOM

AND LOVE

FOR DAYS
WEEKS
AND YEARS

UNTIL ONE DAY
SHE WOKE UP
AND NOTICED
EVERYTHING AROUND HER
HAD CHANGED

THE FUTURE SHE ONCE DREAMED OF
WAS NOW HER LIVED REALITY

"the more i loosen
the grips
on who i think i am
the more i get
to step into
who i am
becoming"

You will make it
through this chapter

The one that cracked
your heart wide open
oozing through every page
is the pain that allows you
to feel again

The chapter that invited you
to stay a little bit longer
than you wanted to

Asking you
to make notes
in its margins

Reading your own words back
filled with tears in your eyes
learning from your
past stories of mistakes
so that you can make the changes
to write a better future

It might be the longest chapter
of the entire book
but I promise you
you will make it through this chapter

WHAT INGREDIENTS (AND WHY) DO YOU WANT TO POUR INTO YOURSELF EVERYDAY TO CREATE YOUR FUTURE REALITY WITH?

HALF OF ME

Acknowledging my truth
has been one of the
hardest initiations
of my life

To admit to myself
that I'd been headed
off course most of my twenties

For too many years
I felt like I was driving
in the wrong lane
going backwards

Feeling guilty
for being unable
to just be grateful
for this beautiful path
I'd already chosen
to walk down

But it was spinning me
in circles
going nowhere

I think that must be
why they say
the truth will set you free

Because now I'm living
in my thirties
with a clearer vision
than I have ever had before

Veering off to drive
in the right lane
going forwards

Forging a path
towards freedom

   HALF OF ME

Forgiving myself
so that I can let go
of this beautiful chapter
and leave it in my past

I trust
it's all been moving me
to the places
I'm meant
to be going

I trust in this now moment

a love letter to Inward Athlete

You were the first thing
I never rushed

We took our time

I breathed you in slowly
carried you
around with me
as I listened
to how you wanted
to tell your story

I held you softly

Cradled you
with only the purest
of intentions
you were my muse for years

Conversations between us
never went stale

I can hear your voice still

Wafting down the halls
on repeat
in my memory

I loved you mercifully

As I wore you
clasped inside a locket
clutched tightly
to my chest

I was the musician
and you were the violin
pulling the bow slowly
across all four of your strings

Our music carried
across the Tuscan Valley together
through the marble buildings
echoing for miles
it was the longest-shortest time
I can ever remember

One day
you asked me to stay
so I let you

I never would have told you
that you were overstaying
your welcome

I still can't tell
if you were my quickest hello
or my longest goodbye

When I think back on us
you remind me of the solstice

The longest day
in the heat of the summer

Sometimes we would drive all night
just to watch the sunrise together
and as the light would begin to shine
on a brand new day
we'd take the longest inhale
and then we would hold our breath
to make a wish

I have to admit
after I met you
I was afraid
to let go
and exhale again

*What if I never knew
another like you?*

*What if wishes never came true
the same way again?*

Yet, deep down
I always had a knowing
that one day
you would get swept away
with the tides
and that makes sense to me
because the ocean
was our favorite place
to spend the day

So I sent you off
as a message in a bottle
just as the high tide
rolled in

And I watched with tears
in my eyes
as you drifted out to sea
and got picked up
in the waves

I bid you farewell
then got on my knees
and thanked the sand

For letting us daydream upon her
during all those summers
when we were together

You let the stars
be your guide
sailing across the ocean
at night
as you made your way
to a new destination

As you washed upon
the coastline
I prayed you would land
into the hands
of new loving strangers

Ones who deeply yearned for guidance
to walk a sovereign path together

For in my message
inside your bottle
all I left was my contact

Then like magic
you brought me my people

*You changed my life
and I'll never forget you*

This poem is a love letter to my business Inward Athlete. I wrote it in a stream of conscious-
ness watching an Italian middle school orchestra play at the Terme Tettuiccio on a magical
night under the stars. As the music played, I sat there and dreamed about sending my new
business, Inward Athlete, out into the world. I am fully trusting in myself to take the leap of
faith into entrepreneurship and serving in my mission in a new way. I also feel called to help
others do the same.

Jen

You have learned
it's okay to disappoint them

To break others' hearts
at the expense
of keeping yours whole

To shatter them
with integrity
let them down easy
to demolish every dream
they wanted you to be
with as much love in your heart
as you can afford them

Because where you're going
they may never understand

And when you're moving
in alignment with your vision

They will respect your courage
to follow your own path

Even if that means
they fall out of your life

So please
*always break others' hearts
at the expense of keeping yours whole*

HALF OF ME

"It took a lot of inner mindset shifts
working with my beliefs
to feel worthy enough
to follow my own dreams.
If I can do it, you can do it too.
I use subconscious reprogramming
techniques, journaling, visualization,
breathwork, and energy work
on a daily basis to connect to
my future self and dreams.
Then I take action on them."

I can't predict
where this love for writing
is meant to take me

All I knows is
that I'm meant to pour myself into it

To overflow
my cup with it

Trust that the rush of water
will create new rivers
that nourish my soul

So I choose to write
until my fingers
can no longer move
or until my heart
can no longer feel
the weight of these words

And maybe I'm not meant to know
what happens next
even if I desperately
want to use my pen
to write the ending

everything
you have
been through

has been
preparing you

for
this
exact
moment

SHE WONDERS
JUST HOW SHE GOT HERE

BECAUSE
IT DIDN'T HAPPEN
OVERNIGHT

HE TOLD HER
*IT WILL HAPPEN
IN THE LONGEST-SHORTEST TIME*

THEN SHE WATCHED
HER ROAD ONCE
PAVED WITH TAR
DISSOLVE BACK INTO
A FIELD OF WILDFLOWERS

SHE DIDN'T BELIEVE HIM
AT THE TIME

AND STILL TODAY
SHE WONDERS
JUST HOW SHE GOT HERE

*Wise words of wisdom from my mentor and
transformational coach Aaron Rose*

What was that one moment?

Where there was a distinct
before and after

The one that drew you in
and spit you out
a completely
different person?

The moment
that took you on a journey
to the depths of the sea
then down
to the core of the Earth
and when you emerged
back towards that light
it transformed your soul?

That moment
so memorable
it burned a polaroid picture
in the back of your mind?

A picture so beautiful
you want to hold onto it forever
and carry it around with you
inside a locket

The one that's always there to remind you
there's still magic in this Universe

A touchstone
to bring you back
to your own beating heart

Back to that feeling
back to that bliss point
back to that vision

What was that one moment?

That where there was distinct before and after

The one that drew you in
and spit you out

A completely
different person?

This poem is dedicated to Rachel Clift. Thank you, Rachel Clift, for that moment in time when you let me cry on your shoulder that day in a beautiful Tuscan Spa as I poured my heart out to you about wanting to birth this book into the world. Thank you for spending the next year with me after that moment, mentoring me to help birth this book into the world.

Jen

my eyes may not
have seen yet

what's on the other side

of this life transition

but my heart

has already felt
the rush of the magic

for what's awaiting me

on the other side

once i commit to going

I was exhausted

Empty yet filled with love

No more tears left
in these eyes to cry

As a sweet release
of unfelt emotions
lifted from my beating chest

Then he came running towards me
holding hands with our little
a boy with curly hair
and gentle wide eyes

He stood prominent
with open arms
as he leaned over
to scoop me up gently

Carried my weak body
to the bed to rest
tucked me in with honor
kneeled by my side
and began to pray over me

He anointed me
as he rubbed my feet
with oils
placed rose petals
one
by
one
on top my body
then let me rest

HALF OF ME

As he honored my sacrifices
I have made
to make it this far
on my journey
back home to self love

On my journey
back home to wholeness

Then they all climbed into bed with me
him
my boy
and my inner child

We are all there together now

A family

As I began to slumber
off to sleep
I promised each one of them
I would be patient
not to fill the space too soon

I promised them
I would meet them again
when I was fully rested
And able to love them
just as much
as I've been remembering
how to love myself

This poem is dedicated to my future family. I wrote this poem after a breathwork journey where I met my future husband, child, and inner child in a meditative state after using my breath to clear out emotions and energy. I can't wait to meet them.

Jen

Here we are

7.9 billion human
walking former stars

7.9 billion human
bodies of stardust
right here
on Mother Earth

God knows
I am no chemist
or some cosmic astrophysicist
but what I do know
is that we are all made
of tiny celestial elements

As science tells us
we are mostly
just carbon-based beings
just a number on a chart
awarded the atomic number six

Yet, it's from this element
we know we must have been
the remains of grieving
dying star pieces
that once exploded
from the heavens

And these are
the raw ingredients
that make us shine today
the building blocks
of a human life
atoms that stem
from our astrological lines
passed down
from our ancestors
in the sky

How else would one explain
that each of our auras
gives of steam
of colorful heated gamma rays
which are deeply felt
yet hardly seen?

All of us
a unique cocktail
of electric vibrant light
co-creating a shine
down here on Earth
for which we ground
our sacred feet

Can't you feel it all?
octillions of vibrating
electric particles
just coursing through your veins

Ya'll
we're just out here
bumping into one another
creating human galactic
friction pain

So, it makes sense to me
that on the day we die
we take a conscious
space led flight
that returns us
to the sky

It must be
so we can rise
above the darkness
and levitate
to cast more light

So the next time you look up
I hope you will remember
why you came

You came on a mission
to embody stardust
your birthright to live
and for lifetimes to claim

This was the first poem I ever wrote and performed at an open mic in January of 2022.

Jen

2023

When I look back on 2023
this was the year
I came fully back to life

This year was my renaissance

The inner work I had done
the prior two years
finally got witnessed
by others in this 3D reality

As magic bursted from my fingertips
finding a steady pen of devotion
that made its way onto printed
pages of a real book

That landed in the hands of others
being read by eyes who had been
praying to find hope in another's
story of redemption

My words mattered

It's the year I
dripped with wealth
as each step forward
carried me deeper into practice
that began to shower
me with experiences of
of synchronicities of
an abundant universe
I can't yet explain
and maybe I don't have to

I used my voice cracking
through years of static
ready to be heard
as my vocal chords vibrated
giving me wings

to sing the praise
to call others forward

This was the year
I finally broke free
from the chains of my childhood
that had once kept me looping
in the dark as I found
myself emerging from
a tunnel to be greeted
by the light

It was the year
all of my old identities
finally fell to the ground

I didn't evolve into
a new version of me
I finally got to live
as the truest version of me

This was the year
I came fully back to life

This year was my renaissance

FOR THE FIRST TIME
IN HER LIFE
SHE'S NOT RUNNING
FROM SOMETHING
SHE'S RUNNING
TOWARDS IT

TOWARDS BLISSFUL
PEACEFUL MOMENTS

THE KIND OF MOMENTS
FOUND IN OPEN FIELDS
OF WILDFLOWERS
WHERE THE SUN
POURS THROUGH THE TREES
AT JUST THE RIGHT ANGLE

SHE'S RUNNING AND JUMPING
INTO THE OPEN ARMS OF SAFETY

THE ARMS
SHE'S WAITED
FOR LIFETIMES
TO FEEL AGAIN

SHE'S RUNNING TOWARDS
HER CHILDLIKE CURIOSITY
AND HER DIVINE
FEMININE POWER

SHE'S RUNNING TOWARDS
A DEEPER KNOWING
HER MISSION TO SERVE
AND IN-THAT
IS HER MISSION TO LOVE

 HALF OF ME

SHE'S RUNNING TOWARDS
A UNION WITH
HER CREATOR
TO FEEL FULLY ALIGNED
MIND
BODY
AND SPIRIT

IRONICALLY
SHE'S FOUND HERSELF
RUNNING RIGHT TOWARDS
THIS PRESENT MOMENT

AND SHE HAS DECIDED
THIS IS THE PLACE
WHERE SHE WOULD LIKE TO
STAY FOREVER

Dear reader, thank you,
for coming on this inward journey with me.
It is my prayer that as you read,
wrote, and colored the pages of this book,
my story helped shift you back home
to your own heart.

- Jen

About the Author

DR. JENNIFER GELLOCK is a poet, transformational guide for heart-led leaders, and the founder of Inward Athlete. She left her job as a full-time professor in May of 2023 to step fully into her role as an entrepreneur and continue on her mission to shift others back home to their hearts. At the age of thirty-one, she burned out her nervous system after living most of her life with unmanaged chronic stress and anxiety. For too many years, she fought against herself, and became emotionally, physically, mentally, and spiritually exhausted from trudging through the resistance of modern life. Then in 2020, she awakened to a higher knowing and surrendered to a path of doing years of inner work that transformed her from the inside-out.

Her own story has led her down a path to help others connect back to their own inner truth. Her work empowers people to become the fullest expression of themselves in this lifetime. In her work today, with personal clients and at her workshops, she uses a range of conscious awareness and mindfulness tools that include: subconscious reprogramming/mindset work, breathwork, journaling/poetry exercises, visualization techniques, energetic hygiene and clearing practices, prayers of surrender and self-love, and her intuitive leadership guidance to shift others back home to their own inner knowing and take action from that place. She has completed coursework and certifications to become a trauma informed practitioner, mental health first aid responder, and experiential teaching and inclusive educator.

Before embarking on the path of entrepreneurship, she spent four years as an Assistant Professor of Sport Management at the University of Tampa and University and the University of North Alabama after receiving her PhD in Sport Leadership in 2019 from Virginia Commonwealth University. She has taught courses of Sport Leadership, Management, Sociology of Sport, and Psychology of Coaching. Before becoming a professor, she worked in college athletics supporting the holistic development of Division I college athletes and coached Division II women's basketball and completed her MBA in Sport Business in 2014. She graduated from the University of Tampa with her bachelors in Physical Education in 2012 and is a native of Westfield Massachusetts. She is a lover of pizza, cats, and 80's movies.

To find out more about how to work with Dr. Gellock you can visit her website at jennifergellock.com and connect with her on instagram @jennifer_gellock

ISBN: 979-8-218-22067-9 (paperback),
979-8-218-22069-3 (hardcover)

Edited by Freydis Lova.
Book design & layout by Rachel Clift.
rcliftpoetry.com

Cover design by Rachel Clift.
Cover Illustration by Laura Clift.
Interior Illustrations (coloring pages) by Laura Clift.
Copyright © 2023 lauraclift.com

First printing edition, 2023.

Jennifer Gellock, P.hD
@jennifer_gellock
inwardathlete.com